POEMS

jesse carreon

POEMS

iUniverse books may be ordered through booksellers or by contacting:

iUniverse
1663 Liberty Drive
Bloomington, IN 47403
www.iuniverse.com
1-800-Authors (1-800-288-4677)

ISBN: 978-1-4917-8542-3 (sc)
ISBN: 978-1-4917-8543-0 (e)

Library of Congress Control Number: 2015921123

Print information available on the last page.

iUniverse rev. date: 12/28/2015

CONTENTS

JANIS 1

THE BIRTHDAY SONG 1

IF I COULD LOVE 2

FOREVER 4

FLOWERS 5

QUESTION 5

FEAR 6

UNTITLED 7

1 VS 168 7

DREAM 10

WHISPER 11

TEARS 12

SPRING 13

DREAMING 14

VOID 16

DEATH 17

UNTITLED 17

TWO MINDS ALIKE 19

OLD GIRLFRIEND 20

DREAMS 20

THOUGHTS 21

MY DEATH 22

REQUEST 23

DEATH 24

MERCY 25

JANIS 25

DESPERATION 26

TIME 27

VACANT 27

A PRAYER 28

WHO 29

ADDICTION 29

STATUE... 30

UNTITLED... 36

HAPPINESS 37

I 40

MY DREAM... 43

MY DAD.. 45

MY BROTHER... 46

JANIS 48

GOLD CRUCIFIX.. 50

MIND 50

HEADLINES.. 51

SIMPLICITY.. 52

MY DESIRE.. 53

SAD DAY 56

DEATH AND LOVE 57

MY BED 59

MAMA... 60

THOUGHTS.. 60

A ROSE 61

LITTLE CREATURES 63

YOU LOST ME 64

SUNSET 68

OUT THE WINDOW... 69

THANKS.. 70

SAD... 73

CRY... 74

YOURSELF... 76

TODAY 78

CRYING 81

TRY TRY 81

SICKNESS 84

NIGHT 85

BAD NEWS FOR MRS. BROWN 91

HONOR MY FRIEND 96

GETTING OLD.. 97

YOUNG MAN... 98

CRYING MAN.. 99

DARK ROOM 100

DAYTIME 100

BIRTH 103

SIN 108

ME 112

THE WORD 113

OFTEN 113

FINISHED...114

SILENCE 115

LAUGH 115

OH GOD 116

UNTITLED...116

BAD DREAM..117

SHELL 118

THE TRINITY..118

THIS WORLD 119

MY WIFE AND KIDS 121

ANGRY...121

FOR JANIS 122

BAD LUCK.. 123

FOR JANIS 124

FUNNY BODIES 127

UNTITLED.. 128

TWILIGHT 128

OUR PROBLEMS... 129

A TREE.. 129

REMEMBRANCE 130

VIRGIN 130

UNDER THE TREE..131

LOOK INTO DARKNESS 131

NO TOY 133

LOVE YOU 134

TOTAL LOVE 142

THOUGHTS..143

SALLY 143

DAYTIME BLUES..145

NO CHANGE 146

FREED..147

7TH BIRTHDAY..148

FRIDAY AFTERNOON 152

WORRY..160

LOST SOUL 161

MEXICAN...162

IDIOT 166

HITCHHIKING 167

BODIES 168

FLOWERS 169

FUNERAL FOR MY FRIEND'S BROTHER 169

CONVERSATION..172

COUNTRY SONG.. 174

UNTITLED..177

john 182

LOVE 184

DEAD DOG 186

CHURCH 187

A MEMORY 187

COLORS # 2...188
FAREWELL..188
BRIGHT MOON 190
QUESTION...190
CONFESSION 191
MY WIFE...192
OLD GIRLFRIEND......................................193
MAKING LOVE TO JANIS 194
A WHITE VINYL.......................................200
DREAMING 201
ME 202
IMMIGRANT 203
EVOLUTION A THOUGHT......................203
TOMORROW 204
DREAM # 104..210
THE LIGHT...212
WHO 218
NO TITLE...220
A THOUGHT WHILE AT WORK...........223
THE WORLD 232
ONCE YOUNG..233
30..235
INFINITY # 10..236
A HUMBLE CHRISTIAN 243
(We take Christ for granted) 243
101 254
KAILA AND GRANDFATHER..................255
LAUGHING 256
UNTITLED...256
DARKNESS...258
#105 259
801 261

FOR MY WIFE.. 270
QUESTION.. 271
LOST FOR WORDS 272
UNTITLED...276
A WARNING 276
TEACHER... 277
MANKIND 279
PR SCHEME 279
DIRT 280
NO CHOICE.. 280
PLAYTIME...281
WEAK... 283
MY SAVIOR 294
YOU 306
DABOO/DAWOO... 308
THE CRUCIFIXION 318

JANIS

EARLY IN MORNING
BEFORE THE ROOSTER CROWS
BEFORE THE SUN AWAKES THE DAY
I THINK OF YOU

THE BIRTHDAY SONG

HE SANG ME A SONG
HE WAS OUT OF TUNE
THE WORDS WERE MUMBLED
MAYBE NO WORDS AT ALL
HE STRAINED
ON THE LOW NOTES
HE STRAINED
ON THE HIGH NOTES
HE STRAINED
TO FINISH THE SONG
A TRILLION MILLION
NOTES HAVE BEEN HEARD
NONE
MORE APPRECIATED
THAN THOSE
STRAINED CRACKED
OUT OF TUNE
SUNG
BY MY BOY
ON MY BIRTHDAY

UNTITLED

YOU
I ALMOST CRIED
I DIDN'T
HOW COULD I
YOU
THE god
I
THE PAWN
I ALMOST CRIED
NOW
I KNOW THE GAME
I WON'T CRY

IF I COULD LOVE

IF
I COULD LOVE
SOMEONE
HALF AS MUCH
AS I LOVE MYSELF
LIFE
WOULD HAVE MORE MEANING
LIFE
WOULD BE MORE TOLERABLE
IF
I COULD LOVE
I CANNOT

AN INVITATION

I
INVITE MY FRIENDS
TO PAY ME
A LAST VISIT
ONE
WITH SONG AND DANCE
JUMP AND SHOUT
LOUD IF YOU WILL
SO I MAY HEAR
DON'T CRY
PLEASE DON'T CRY
IF YOU MUST MOURN
MOURN FOR YOURSELF
WHO HAVE YET
TO LEAVE THIS DUNGEON
YES
YOU
ARE WELCOME
TO
MY GREATEST
CELEBRATION

HA HA HA

DEATH
HA HA HA
LIFE
I CALLED YOUR BLUFF
ONCE
THAT'S ENOUGH
HAPPINESS
HAS FINALLY COME
WITHOUT REGRETS
I LEAVE MY CELL
KNOWING
I'VE DONE MY JOB WELL

FOREVER

I WILL LOVE YOU
FOREVER
I SPEAK TO YOU
FROM MY GRAVE
MY DARK AND DAMP
BED
I CAN SEE YOU
THOUGH
MY EYES ARE CLOSED FOREVER
AT NIGHT
WHEN YOU LIE IN BED ALONE
WHEN MY MEMORIES
BRING TEARS TO YOUR EYES
I TOO
CRY

FLOWERS

I LOVE
    TO SMELL
    TO SEE
    TO TOUCH
THEM
WILL YOU
BE
MY FLOWER

© copyright 2010 Jesse Carreon

QUESTION

HAVE YOU HEARD
THE CRY
OF A FALLING TREE
HAVE YOU HEARD
THE CRY
OF A BABY
HAVE YOU LISTENED
IS THERE
A DIFFERENCE
ARE THEY NOT
BOTH
A CRY FOR
HELP

© copyright 2010 Jesse Carreon

MOTHER NATURE

AH
MOTHER NATURE
SHE
LOOKS GOOD TODAY
TALL GREEN TREES
BEAUTIFUL FLOWERS
BLUE SKIES
GENTLE BREEZE
AH
SHE IS
A
BEAUTIFUL WOMAN
HER ONE BLEMISH
MAN

FEAR

I AM NOT
AN ADMIRER
OF LIFE
NOR AM I ANXIOUS
FOR DEATH
I DREAM AND EXIST
IN A LIMBO
TIRED OF LIFE
SCARED OF DEATH
IF I COULD
I WOULD BE
A ROCK OR A TREE
IF NOT
A DOG
THAT'S OK WITH ME

UNTITLED

LOOK IN THE SKY
LOOK
WAY UP HIGH
THERE
ON THE OTHER SIDE
OF THE MILKY WAY
THERE
IS WHERE I LIVE
THERE
IS WHERE
I BELONG

© copyright 2010 Jesse Carreon

1 VS 168

VISITING GOD ON SUNDAYS
I FIND IT HARD TO SIT
ONE HOUR PER WEEK
INSIDE YOUR TEMPLE
I CAN IMAGINE
HOW YOU MUST FEEL
GIVING ME
167 HOURS A WEEK
THANK YOU

© copyright 2010 Jesse Carreon

A DREAM

I HAD A DREAM LAST NIGHT
I SAW DEATH
HIS RIGHT HAND HELD POWER
HIS LEFT HAND HELD WEALTH
HE NEVER SMILED
THE FACE LOOKED FAMILIAR
    IT'S BEEN A LONG TIME SINCE YOU LOOKED
IN A MIRROR
    A QUIETENED VOICE CRIED
HELP HELP CRIED I
DEATH BEGAN EATING AN APPLE PIE
THE MIND WILLING THE BODY NOT
MY SOUL CRIED OUT
FIGHT
A SILLY SMILE AN EVIL GRIN
DEATH KNEW HE'D WIN
HE ATE ANOTHER PIECE OF PIE
THE FACE LOOKED FAMILIAR
    IT'S BEEN A LONG TIME SINCE YOU LOOKED
IN A MIRROR
    A QUIETENED VOICE CRIED
THE id IS A SELFISH ANIMAL
HARD TO SATISFY
THE MORE YOU WANT THE MORE YOU SEE
AN ENDLESS PIT
DEATH'S SILLY GRIN
SENT CHILLS DOWN MY SPINE
BLINDERS ARE VERY EFFECTIVE
TUNNEL VISION

IS SOMETIME VERY USEFUL
THE FACE LOOKED FAMILIAR
    IT'S BEEN A LONG TIME SINCE YOU LOOKED
IN A MIRROR
    A QUIETENED VOICE CRIED
WITHOUT WARNING
HE CALLED MY NAME
WITH A WAVE OF HIS HAND
HE REMOVED THE HAZE
IT WAS THEN I KNEW
WE WERE ONE AND THE SAME
I TRIED TO SMILE INSTEAD
I CRIED
NO USE IN WONDERING
WHY
I AWOKE FROM MY DREAM
WITH A HOWLING SCREAM
I WILL AWAIT MY FATE
TOMORROW

WILL YOU

WILL YOU
SPEND SOME TIME WITH ME
I'LL PAINT
BOTH
THE SUN AND THE SEA
WITH COLORS YOU
HAVE NEVER SEEN
AND
IF IN TIME
THE COLORS FADE
I'LL NOT CRY
WHEN YOU WALK AWAY

DREAM

I SHOULD NOT CRY
FOR A FLOWER
WHO HAS NOT
KNOWN LIFE
THUS
WILL NOT KNOW
DEATH
I WILL DREAM
OF ITS BEAUTY

SUMMER BREEZE

SUMMER BREEZE
GENTLY TEASING
THE LEAVES
ON A TREE
WITH THE RHYTHM
AND AFFECTION
OF A MAN
FOR HIS WOMAN

© copyright 2010 Jesse Carreon

WHISPER

COULD I WHISPER
A FEW WORDS
A FEW OF PRAISE
A FEW OF THANKS
ONE OF LOVE
SO
WHEN THE TIME COMES
AS
I KNOW IT WILL
WE GO
OUR SEPARATE WAYS
I MAY BECOME A PART OF YOU
AS
YOU BECOME A PART OF ME
AND
THAT BOND WE SHARED
WILL EVOKE THE ENVY
OF ALL THE gods
AND
ALL THEIR creations

© copyright 2010 Jesse Carreon

RAINDROPS

THE BEAUTY OF SNOW
IN NOT APPRECIATED
UNLESS VIEWED
ON AN OPEN FIELD
THE BEAUTY
OF RAINDROPS
FALLING
    A GENTLE SONG PLAYED
ON A METAL COVER
IS NOT APPRECIATED
UNLESS HEARD
WITH YOUR WOMAN
IN BED

TEARS

COMING DOWN MY CHEEK
MY MIND KNOWS WHY IT WEEPS
MY HEART WILL
WAIT FOR A BRIGHTER DAY
FOR NOW
THE CLOUDS WILL NOT
GO AWAY

BLIND

'TIS
DARK BEFORE MY EYES
THOUGHT MANY SWEAR
I HAVE THE EYES
OF AN EAGLE
NO MATTER
HOW HARD I TRY
TRUTH
TRUTH I CANNOT FIND

SPRING

TREES SWAYING
IN THE BREEZE
BIRDS SINGING
BOYS AND GIRLS
AT THE PARK
A COLD CAN OF BEER
AND
I
IN MY HOLE
BENEATH
SO DARK

THE MASK

I WEAR A MASK
TO HIDE MYSELF FROM ME
MY PAINTED FACE
BETTER LIKED
BY
THE HUMAN RACE
AND
LIKE ALL
US
SILLY CLOWNS
I SELDOM SMILE
BUT
WILL ALWAYS FROWN

DREAMING

AS
I SIT
DREAMING OF A PEACEFUL EARTH
THE WORLD AROUND ME CRUMBLES
I
CLOSE MY EYES
SO
THE TEARS
WONT FALL

INCEST

INCEST
OR THE MOTHER
WAS GANG RAPED
SOMEONE WAS
SCREWED
I BELIEVE IT WAS BY HER SONS
DAMN YOU
DAMN YOU MAN
DAMN YOU
INTELLIGENCE
SISTER WATER
FORCED TO CARRY
YOUR WASTE
BROTHER AIR
KEPT IN CHECK
WITH A STEADY DIET OF SMOG
MOTHER EARTH
HER BEAUTIFUL FACE
SCARRED AND MUTILATED
AND
IN SHAME
WE TRY OUR BEST
TO HIDE HER SCARS
WITH JEWELS
OF
CONCRETE GLASS AND STEEL

SMILE

SMILE
HOW CAN YOU ASK ME TO SMILE
LOOK AT THE WORLD
LOOK AT MAN
YOU ASK ME
TO SMILE
WHAT'S WRONG WITH YOU
ARE YOU SICK

VOID

I SEE MYSELF
A VOID
FLOATING OUT
IN SPACE
PAST INFINITY
INTO
NEVER NEVER
LAND
THERE
I WILL FIND
THE gods
I WILL ASK
WAS IT
IN A DRUNKEN
RAGE
you CREATED
THE HUMAN RACE

DEATH

AH
DEATH WHY THE SMILE
PLEASE WAIT
WAIT
FOR JUST A LITTLE WHILE
FOR I FEAR THE PRICE
I HAVE TO PAY
I FEAR THE DAY
WHEN TOMORROW IS TODAY
AND TODAY IS TOMORROW

UNTITLED

I CANNOT SEE
WITH BLIND EYES
I CANNOT HEAR
WITH DEAF EARS
I CANNOT LOVE
IF I HAVE NO LOVE
I WILL SLEEP
HOPING TO AWAKE
IN A DIFFERENT WORLD

DREAM

I HAD A DREAM LAST NIGHT
A DREAM
ONE OF FRIGHT
I DREAMT
I WAS STANDING
STANDING
NAKED
ALL ALONE
ALONE
INSIDE THE ASTRODOME
BEEN STONED BEEN STONED
I COULD HAVE BORNE ALL THE PAIN
I COULD HAVE BORNE ALL THE SORROW
IF NOT BY ACCIDENT
OUT OF THE CORNER OF MY EYE
HAD
I NOT NOTICED
JESUS
ALL DRESSED IN WHITE
SELLING
COKE POPCORN
AND
BEER
(I was inspired by a tv preacher)

SHE

SHE LIES ENTERTAINED
BY HER DREAMS
THE MIRROR REFLECTION
OF HER SOFT AND GENTLE PROMISE
GIVES JOY TO THE
DARKNESS OF THE DAY
LOOK
NOT TOUCHING
   AT THAT
   WHICH CANNOT BE MINE
IF FATE
COULD BE TEMPTED
TEMPT IT I WOULD
AND ASK
FOR THE DREAM
TO LAST FOREVER

TWO MINDS ALIKE

IT IS NOT I
OUT OF SEQUENCE
THIS ANGRY WORLD
TRAVELS A WELL WORN ROAD
DO NOT CRY MURDER
WHEN IT IS YOU
HOLDING THE LOADED
GUN
I AM
A MAN OF PEACE

OLD GIRLFRIEND

SHE HAS COMPROMISED
SHE IN HER NEW WAY OF LIFE
LOST IN A DREAM
FULL OF LIES
AND
JUST LIKE THE TREES
IN EARLY FALL
SHE WILL SHED
HER DREAMS
HOPES AND ALL

DREAMS

A GOOD DREAM
A BAD DREAM
A LIVE DREAM
A SICK DREAM
A DEAD DREAM
THE LAST IS MINE

DAWN

I LOOK FORWARD
TO DAWN EACH DAY
IT IS THE TIME
WHEN MY
    CONCENTRATION IS HIGH
    DESIRES RUN LOOSE
    THE AIR IS FRESH
    THE CITY SEEMS DEAD
DAWN
CAN BE INSPIRING
DAWN
CAN BE ENLIGHTENING
DAWN
CAN BE DANGEROUS
IT IS THE TIME
NIGHT KISSES DAY

© copyright 2010 Jesse Carreon

THOUGHTS

LIKE THE CLOUDS
IN THE SKY
THEY ROAM
NO REASON WHY
WITHOUT SHAPE
SOMETIMES SO CLEAR

CRY

I WOULD CRY
I'VE RUN OUT OF TEARS
LIFE IS NOT A BUNDLE OF JOY
I WOULD LIKE TO AWAKE
FIND A NEW SUN SHINING
I KNOW I WILL NOT
SO WHY WASTE YOUR TIME AND MINE
TELLING YOU OF MY DREAMS

MY DEATH

AS THE STARS DIED
I STOOD
WATCHING
WONDERING
WILL THE HEAVENS TREMBLE
AT MY DEATH
NO
MY DEATH LIKE
THE SHOOTING STAR
SEEN BY FEW
WILL BE NOTICED
BY
ONLY A FEW
SO TELL
    THE SUN
    THE MOON
    THE EARTH
NOT
TO AWAIT MY DEATH

JFK GOT SHOT

I AIN'T NEVER
DID HAVE NO HERO
ONCE
I ALMOST DID
BANG
BANG CRIED THE GUN
OH GOD CRIED MAN
AS HE FELL
OH OH OH
SAID I
AS THE TV IMAGE
RETURNED BACK TO
ITS REGULAR PROGRAMMING

REQUEST

DEATH WOULD YOU MIND
IF I ASKED FOR MORE TIME
TIME ENOUGH
TO MAKE MY LIFE
WORTH LIVING
I WILL NOT
BE GREEDY
I WISH
ONLY AN EVENING

MY SON

MY 25 POUNDS OF ENERGY
THE NEXT GENERATION
A FUTURE LEADER
POLITICAL
SCIENTIFIC
SOCIAL
THE NEXT LINK
IN MY FAMILY TREE
A STEPPING STONE
FOR FATHER TIME
FOR THE MOMENT
MY ARCH ENEMY
BATTLING FOR POSSESSION
OF MY PENCIL

DEATH

DEATH
I SHUDDER WHEN
I THINK OF YOU
I CANNOT SEE
PAST THE DARKNESS
YOU BRING
IF SOME WAY
I COULD
WISH MYSELF
PAST YOU
I WOULD

MERCY

WOE IS ME
CANT YOU SEE
I AM A FOOL
TRYING TO GET A THRILL
A THRILL
A THRILL
BIG DEAL
WHAT IS LIFE
    AN EMPTY CAN
ON A PILE OF JUNK

JANIS

TO YOU FROM ME
A FEW WORDS
TO EXPRESS MY
LOVE
I GIVE YOU
MY LIFE

LOVERS

LOVERS
WALKING IN THE PARK
CHILDREN
SINGING A HAPPY SONG
I
WONDERING
WHERE I BELONG
SOMEDAY
I
KNOW NOT WHEN
SHE
WILL COME
HOLD MY HAND
AND
LIKE THE FLOWERS
IN EARLY SPRING
YOU KNOW
I WILL BLOOM
AGAIN

DESPERATION

LIFE IS A DREAM
A BAD DREAM
MAN IS A JOKE
A BAD JOKE
HEAVEN
IS THE EXCUSE
FOR KEEPING
THE DREAM AND THE JOKE
GOING

TIME

TIME
SO THEY SAY
IS INFINITE
TIME
SUBSERVIENT
TO NO ONE
TIME
COUNTS AS
ITS FRIEND
GOD

VACANT

I FEEL VACANT
I FEEL ABANDONED
I FEEL PAIN
I FEEL COLD STEEL
AGAINST MY TEMPLE
CLICK
EMPTY CHAMBER
TODAY
IS NOT MY DAY

STONE

I ASKED FOR LOVE
AND GOT STONED
I ASKED FOR PEACE
AND GOT STONED
SO
I GOT STONED
FOUND MY
LOVE AND PEACE
BOTH
WITHIN MY MIND

A PRAYER

I THANK YOU
FOR MY LIFE
YOUR LAWS
ARE HARD TO UNDERSTAND
MUCH HARDER TO FOLLOW
IF I FALL
IF I FIND IT
HARD TO STAND
IF AT TIMES
I GIVE UP
IF AT TIMES
I CRY OUT
IN ANGER
FORGIVE ME
I AM HUMAN
I LOVE YOU

WHO

I DON'T MISS YOU
LIKE I THOUGHT
I WOULD
THIS BROKEN HEART
WILL BE WELL
GIVE IT TIME
IN THE MORNINGS
WHEN THE SUN CHASES
DARKNESS AWAY
WHEN THE COLD COLD WIND
MAKES
ME STAY IN BED
IT IS THEN
I MISS YOU THE
MOST

ADDICTION

LOOK
DON'T TELL ME OF
HELL
I'VE SEEN IT
LIKED IT
AND
I AIN'T
DEAD

WAR

WAR
IS NOT HELL
IT MAKES MONEY
FOR MANY
FOR OTHERS
IT GIVES THEM
PEACE

STATUE

IF I WERE
A god
I WISH ME
TO BE
A
MARBLE STATUE
NO HEART
NO RESPONSIBILITY
ALL SHOW

AUSTIN REVISITED

THE SUN WAS SHINING
AND I
FOOL THAT I AM
SMILED
A FRIEND CAME BY
TO SAY HI
HAVE A CUP
SAID I
THANKS SAID HE
THE WEATHERMAN
HAD FORECAST RAIN
NATURE HAD FOOLED US
AGAIN
TECHNOLOGY IS A TOOL
NOT A FORCE
MOTHER NATURE SINGS
ANY SONG SHE
PLEASES
WE DRANK COFFEE
MY FRIEND AND I
ARGUED
SHAKESPEARE
ARISTOTLE
CHRIST
JOHN LENNON TOO
NIGHT
REPLACED DAY
MY FRIEND

SAID GOODBYE
I SAT DOWN
POURED
ONE LAST CUP
TURNED THE RADIO ON
VIETNAM
RAPE
THE SHAME OF MUNICH 1972
THE COFFEE
HAD TURNED
COLD AND BITTER

WAR

I COULD SMELL
THE RAIN
WHEN MY FEET
TOUCHED
THE GREEN GRASS
I KNEW
THE HEAVENS
REFLECTED
AS IF BY MAGIC
MADE A BLUE HOLE
IN THE FIELD OF GREEN
ALL AROUND
I COULD HEAR
THE BOMBS
FUNNY
CHILDREN DON'T CRY
WHEN THEY DIE
FAR AWAY
THE SECRET CRY OF A BIRD
CALLING ITS MATE
MY EYES FORGOT
MY MIND WOULD NOT
THE BURNING CHILD
WITH EYES SO WILD
I
IN MY SUIT OF GREEN
NOW
IN MY PRIVATE
HELL

I MUST REMEMBER
A BLIND MAN CANNOT
SEE
A DEAF MAN CANNOT
HEAR
A SAD MAN CANNOT
SMILE
AND I
HAVE NO EXCUSE

MY SON

I FORGOT
YOU
ARE JUST A BOY
I SAW IT
IN YOUR EYES
READY TO TAKE
THE WORLD
OFTEN
I KNOW I AM
RESTRICTIVE AND STERN
IF AT TIMES I SEEM
ANGRY AND CONFUSED
I AM
I'VE BEEN ASKED TO MOLD
YOU
FROM A BOY INTO A MAN
I
FEAR NOT FOR ME
IT IS YOU
WHO
WILL HAVE TO PAY
THE PRICE
OF MY FAILURE

© copyright 2010 Jesse Carreon

THOUGHT

BEFORE THE BREAK
OF DAWN
I SIT
WITH THE
TREES, FLOWERS, AND GOD
MY EMPTY LIFE
WELL AMPLIFIED
MY FALSE SMILE
EXPOSED

UNTITLED

THERE ARE MANY WONDERS
IN THE UNIVERSE
FROM
THE SMALLEST SUBATOMIC PARTICLE
TO THE VASTNESS OF ALL CREATION
THANK YOU MR. HUBBLE
FROM
THE ENERGY OF
A GENTLE BREEZE
TO THE ENERGY WITHIN
THE BUILDING BLOCKS OF CREATION
NOTHING COMPARES
TO THE
BIRTH OF MAN

TREES

I AM PART
OF THE TREES
I AM PART
OF THE SKIES AND SEAS
WHEN THEY DIE
A PART OF ME
WILL DIE
WHEN I DIE
A PART OF THEM
WILL DIE
WE ARE ALL
A PART
OF
GOD'S CREATION

HAPPINESS

A NEW CAR
LITTLE BIT
OF MONEY
A NEW GIRL
EACH DAY

LOST SON

I LOST HIM
I LOST HIM
HE DID NOT
ASK
MY NAME
HE DID NOT
CRY
FOR HELP
HIS EYES
SAID IT
ALL
I MUST PAY
FOR
MY MISTAKES
THE PRICE
IS
HIGH

I STAND

I STAND ALONE
TREMBLING
AT THE THOUGHTS
WITHIN MY MIND
TORN
MY BELIEFS AND NEEDS
OPPOSED
I STAND ALONE
MY MIND RUNNING
AN ENDLESS RACE
MY SOUL
WORKING HARD
TO EARN
ITS GRACE
I STAND ALONE
NO HELP
JUST I
I MUST MAKE
THE CHOICE

A GIRL AT THE AIRPORT

SHE STANDS
ALONE
A PEBBLE BY THE SEA
UNNOTICED
WAITING TO BOARD
HER PLANE
HUMANITY FLOATING BY
AN
UNCARING RUSHING SEA
SHE STANDS
ALONE
ENDANGERED

I

THE DESERT
AN EMPTY HOUSE
A BOMBED CITY
A BURNED FOREST
AN EMPTY CAN OF BEER
SUCH
AM I

HELP

HELP ME
HELP ME
HELP ME
A MAN'S
LAST SUPPER
HELP ME
HELP ME
HELP ME
CLANG
OF A METAL
DOOR
HELP ME
HELP ME
HELP ME
FLICKERING LIGHTS
OF A CELL
HELP ME
HELP ME
HELP ME
A NOOSE DANGLES
HELP ME
HELP ME
HELP ME
GOD HELP
THE SINNER

STATEMENT

NOT YET A WOMAN
SURELY
NOT A CHILD
I LIKE YOUR SMILE
I LIKE TO KEEP YOU
FOR
A LITTLE WHILE
I LIKE THE SILLY THING
YOU DO
DON'T ASK WHY
ANOTHER DAY ANOTHER TIME
ONCE
I MIGHT HAVE ASKED
STAY BE MINE
TODAY
I RATHER HAVE YOU
AS
A HAPPY MOMENT
ON MY LONESOME ROAD
TO DEATH

LOST MIND

I HAVE MISPLACED
MY MIND
I THOUGHT
I LOANED IT TO MY
HEAD
I HAVE LOOKED
FAR AND WIDE
TO NO AVAIL
NO NEED TO WORRY
THIS PROBLEM
IS NOT MINE
EXCLUSIVELY

MY DREAM

I'VE PLACED
MY DREAMS
IN THE HANDS OF MAN
WITH WHOM
I HOPE TO SOMEDAY
SHARE
LOVE
PEACE
WORK

MY LADY JANIS

I ENJOY
LAYING MY BODY
NEXT TO YOU
I ENJOY
THE WAY
YOU TOUCH ME
I ENJOY
SEEING YOUR
NAKED BODY
I ENJOY
KNOWING YOU
THE WAY I DO
I ENJOY
CALLING YOU
MY WIFE
I ENJOY
KNOWING YOU
AS MY LOVER
BEST OF ALL
I ENJOY
YOUR LOVE

CRY AGAIN

I CRY
THE SUN SHINES
SILENTLY
THE ROAR
OF ITS RAYS
STRIKING
MY BODY
RESEMBLES
THE SADNESS
IN MY HEART
I CRY

MY DAD

HE AND I
WERE OPPOSITE
YET MUCH
THE SAME
HE SAW BLACK
I SAW WHITE
HE SAW RAIN
I SAW SUNSHINE
HE SAW THIS
I SAW THAT
THIS SCHISM
KEPT US
FAR APART
TWO BULLS
OPPOSED
HEAD TO HEAD
NO REASON
WHY

MY BROTHER

I REMEMBER
LATE SEPTEMBER DAYS
WHEN
HE AND I
WOULD PLAY
COWBOY GAMES
GOOD GUY BAD GUY
TOGETHER
TILL LATE DAY
I REMEMBER
OUR TEEN YEARS
COMPETITION AND FIGHTS
ALWAYS TOGETHER
HE AND I
WE PARTED
HE AND I
HE GOT MARRIED
NOT I
SEPARATED
FOREVER
WHO IS TO SAY
I DO NOT MISS
HIM
EACH AND EVERY DAY

MOM AND DAD

I LIKE TO SAY
A FEW WORDS
ABOUT
TWO SIMPLE PEOPLE
TWO PEOPLE
WHOM
I HAVE NOT MENTION
I HAVE A WIFE
AND CHILDREN
THEY DID NOT
GIVE ME LIFE
LIKE
THAT OLD MAN AND WIFE
FUNNY
A BUSY MIND FORGETS
DAYS TURNS TO YEARS
TIME FLIES
I MAY NOT HAVE THEM
IN MIND
THEY NEVER LEFT
MY HEART

© copyright 2010 Jesse Carreon

AFRAID

I AIN'T AFRAID
TO DIE
I HAVE CONVINCED
ALL
EXCEPT I

© copyright 2010 Jesse Carreon

JANIS

EARLY
BEFORE THE SUN
AWAKES THE DAY
AFTER
THE PASSIONS
HAVE SUBSIDED
TOGETHER WE LAY
TILL THE SOUND
OF YOUR BEATING
HEART
MINGLES
WITH THE SOUNDS
OF DAY

© copyright 2010 Jesse Carreon

DRINKING WATER

I HAD STOPPED
FOR
A DRINK OF WATER
WHEN I NOTICED
BUZZING FLIES
BUZZING OVER
ANIMAL DROPPINGS
STARING
SUDDENLY
BEFORE MY EYES
I SAW HUMANITY
BUZZING WILDLY
STRONGLY ATTRACTED
TO THIS WORLD
BIG HOUSE
SHINING CAR
PLASTIC WOMEN
EMPTY DREAMS
ME FIRST
BLIND
BLIND
TO SORROW
BLIND
BLIND
TO ALL
EXCEPT THE MIRROR
I FINISHED MY DRINK
GAVE THANKS
WALKED AWAY
WITH A BETTER
VIEW
OF THIS WORLD

GOLD CRUCIFIX

THE DEAD MAN
ON THE CROSS
HANGS
HATED DESPISE
MOST OF ALL
BE DEAD
MAN SHOOTING DICE
A SHATTERED BODY
A TORN HEART
A PROMISED KEPT
HANGS
HANGS IN SILENCE
WHILE YOU AND I
CHASE
EMPTY DREAMS

MIND

THE INSIDE OF MY MIND
REEKS
OF OLD AGE AND TIME
IDEAS
ARE STAGNANT
THOUGHT
LONG CEASED TO FLOW
DISILLUSION DESPERATION
IS A
DEAD END ROAD

HEADLINES

NEWSPAPERS
CRY OUT
BLOODY REVOLUTION
ALL FILLED WITH BURNING HATE
WELL SANITIZED
NOT MADE CLEAR
WELL HIDDEN
TO YOU
THE PRICE
FATHERS
MOTHERS
SONS AND DAUGHTERS
WHO PAY
WITH BLOOD
THEY LIVE
THEIR LIVES
IN DIRT AND FILTH
WHILE YOU
AND I
DRINK
OUR MORNING COFFEE
ON TABLES WITH COVERS
OH
SO WHITE

MY WRITINGS

A WRITER
I MAY NOT BE
NOR ARE THE BIRDS
NOR ARE THE FLOWERS
NOR IS THE SUN
NEVER WOULD
I FORFEIT
ONE
WITHOUT ONE
MY LIFE
WOULD BE LESS

© copyright 2010 Jesse Carreon

SIMPLICITY

WILL SET ME FREE
AN UNCOMPLICATED MIND
A FREE MIND
HOPE LOVE DEATH
THIS IS ALL I SEEK
NO LESS
NO MORE

© copyright 2010 Jesse Carreon

TIME

STAND STILL
STILL AS A TREE
ON A WINDLESS DAY
WHILE MY
MIND
TRANSVERSES
THE INFINITE
THROUGH AND BEYOND
THE BEAUTY AND WONDERS
OF CREATION
TO LIFE
ITSELF

MY DESIRE

I DESIRE
TO BE ALONE
NOT TO BELONG
TO A GIVEN
SET OF NORMS
I'D
RATHER BE AN IDEA
WITH INFINITY
AS
MY ONLY
MASTER

THE BAND

MY SO-CALLED FRIENDS
THEY SMILE
SHAKE MY HAND
THEY CANNOT UNDERSTAND
THEY ARE A PLASTIC BAND
STANDING BELOW MY IRON HAND
DANCE AND SING YOUR SONG
I KNOW I DON'T
BELONG
YOUR DREAMS
FULL
OF HATE AND FEAR
SING YOUR SONG
AIR YOUR FEARS
WHILE
OTHERS SHED TEARS
TRYING
HARD TO CONTROL
MY HATE
I KNOW A TIME WILL COME
YOUR DREAM AND SONG
WILL DIE AWAY
LIKE THE PLASTIC BAND
YOU ARE
I'LL SIT YOU DOWN
WALK AWAY

DREAM #3

I AWOKE KINDA EARLY
MISSED THE LAST HALF
OF MY DREAM
I FELT A HAND ON MY EYES
MY MIND GOT UP TO SCREAM
I SAW THE MORNING PAPER
AND
TO MY SURPRISE
IN BOLD NEWS LETTERS
ADVERTISING
THE SECOND COMING
OF CHRIST
AMONG A WILD
CELEBRATION
STOOD TWO NATIONS
BOTH IN A STRANGE
CONFUSION
TO MY RIGHT STOOD
THOSE DRESSED IN WHITE
TO MY LEFT
THOSE
TRYING THEIR BEST
TO HIDE

FOR SCOTT

SON
I THINK
YOU ARE
THE MOST IMPORTANT
MAN
IN THIS WORLD
LET
ME TELL YOU
I LOVE YOU

SAD DAY

IS THERE
A MAGIC
WAND
ONE
WHICH WOULD
LET THE MIRROR
SAY
YOU DID
YOUR BEST
TODAY

JANIS

A WORD OF LOVE
I
A PART OF YOU
YOU
A PART OF ME
US
OUR CHILDREN
LIFE
LOVE EXPRESSED

DEATH AND LOVE

OUR LOVE
IS MUCH GREATER
THAN DEATH
I WILL AWAIT
FOR THAT HAPPY DAY
WHEN YOU
JOIN ME

THE KNIGHT

WHERE
DID THEY GO
THOSE DREAMS
OF EARLY YEARS
ONE FOR ME
ONE FOR MY FAMILY
ONE FOR THE WORLD
ONE FOR HUMANITY
WHAT HAPPENED TO
THAT BRAVE BRAVE
KNIGHT
WHO
FOREVER SWORE TO
FIGHT
FOR
JUSTICE HONOR
AND THE POOR
HE DIED

THE WIND

I AM LIKE THE WIND
RAMBLING
ON AND ON
FOREVER
YOU CAN FEEL
MY PRESENCE
YET
NOT SEE ME
AT NIGHT
WHEN THE MOON
IS HIGH
I AM
THE DIFFERENCE
OF YOU
KNOWING
OR
NOT KNOWING
LOVE

MY BED

I SPEAK TO YOU
FROM MY GRAVE
MY DARK AND DAMP BED
I CAN SEE YOU
THOUGH MY EYES ARE CLOSED FOREVER
AT NIGHT
WHEN YOU LIE IN BED ALONE
WHEN MY MEMORIES
BRING TEARS TO YOUR EYES
I TOO
CRY

MAMA

MAMA MAMA
IS THE CRY OF THE CHILD
PAPA PAPA
THE WORDS HEARD
MAMA MAMA
HOUSE TO HOUSE
PAPA PAPA
IT'S NOT HOME
MAMA PAPA
NO
NOT ANYMORE
MAMA PAPA
THEY ARE THE PRODUCT
OF THE DIVORCE COURT

THOUGHTS

A PLEASANT THOUGHT
ENTERED MY MIND
SENT BY WHO
THE DIVINE
PIERCING LIGHT
EXPOSING
THAT DARKEN PIT
ILLUMINATING
THAT CREATURE CALLED
ID
IF THE MIRROR
COULD BE ERASED
MAYBE THESE TEARS
WOULD VANISH
FROM MY FACE

A ROSE

I SAW A ROSE DIE
TODAY
I LAUGHED I DIDN'T KNOW
WHAT TO SAY
A BIRD CRIED GO AWAY
NO MORE JOKES TODAY
I WALKED
HOPING TO FIND MY WAY
LIFE
ANGLES AND CURVES
NOT A STRAIGHT LINE
SEEING WITH OPAQUE EYES
A ROSE
ONCE IN BLOOM
NOW DEAD AND DOOMED
FAR AWAY
A CHIRPING BIRD
AGREED WITH ME

CHILD

SHE IS A CHILD
SHE IS A WOMAN
WITH CHILD
SHE HAS THE BODY
OF A WOMAN
SHE IS A CHILD
SHE READS MAGAZINES
TV TIMES
PEOPLE
NOT
SHAKESPEARE NOR CROMWELL
SHE KNOWS
WELL
ALL THE HOLLYWOOD STARS
THE YOUNG AND FLASHY
TV HEROES
ASK HER
OF "CAPTAIN AND TENNILLE"
"KC AND THE SUNSHINE BAND"
NOT OF
BEETHOVEN NOR BRAHMS
SHE HUNGERS
TO BE A WOMAN
WELL VERSED IN THE WAYS
OF THE WORLD
HER YEARS BETRAY HER
SHE IS A ROSE BUD
NOT
A ROSE IN FULL BLOOM
THERE IS HOPE

LITTLE CREATURES

I ENVY YOU
YOU WITHOUT
SOUL OR MIND
YOU
WHO WALK THROUGH
LIFE
EAT AND DIE
SIMPLE CREATURES
YOU ARE
NO
CARS, TRAINS NOR AIRPLANES
NO
WARS, BOMBS NOR GUNS
LUCKY US
WE SAY
WE GOT BRAINS AND CHOICE
OH YEAH OH YEAH
LUCKY US (HEE HEE HEE)

SIT

I SIT
TRYING HARD
HARD TO COMPROMISE
THOSE
HALF TRUTHS
MOST KNOW
AS LIES
I SIT
TRYING HARD
HARD TO COMPROMISE
DEATH
AND
LIFE
I SIT I SIT
I CRY

YOU LOST ME

YOU LOST ME
LAST NIGHT
WHEN BY MISTAKE
OR DESIGN
YOU ATTEMPTED
TO TAKE CONTROL
OF MY LIFE
I SEEK SOMEONE
TO ENJOY
WITHOUT PAYING DUES
I NEED
NO CRUTCH

TORTILLIAS Y FRIJOLES

WE WERE FIVE BORN
ONE
FRANK   DIED
MOTHER   DAD
WE WERE SIX TOTAL
DAD WORKED
MOTHER CLEANED HOUSE
WE, HIS HOPES, WENT TO SCHOOL
WE WERE HAPPY
WE WERE POOR
OUR HOUSE WAS SMALL
FOUR ROOMS
DIRT ROAD
JOHNSON GRASS, SNAKES, SPIDERS AND FROGS
SUMMERS WERE HOT
WINTERS COLD
RAIN
A MUDDY ROAD
WE WERE HAPPY
WE WERE POOR
TIME STANDS STILL
NO
THE YOUNG BECOME OLD
THE CHILD A MAN
WE WERE HAPPY
WE WERE POOR

© copyright 2010 Jesse Carreon

A TWIG ON A TREE

MY MIND
LAST NIGHT
WAS RESTLESS
MY SOUL
MUCH THE SAME
DREAMS
THEY WERE FRIGHTENING
DREAMS
OF HOLOCAUST AND PAIN
I SAW
THE LAND ALL RAVISHED
I SAW
MANKIND IN PAIN
WINDS
BLEW FROM ALL DIRECTIONS
BRIMSTONE
MUCH THE SAME
AMONGST THIS
STOOD A RIDER
A MAN OF NOBILITY
DRESSED
IN SILK AND FEATHERS
COLORS
WHITE GOLD AND GREEN
HE
THE SHINY BEACON
AMONG A SWIRLING SEA
HIS FACE
FULL OF ANGER
HIS EYES
FILLED WITH HATE
IN THE NAME OF JUSTICE
HE HURLED
WIND AND BRIMSTONE

IN THE NAME OF HONOR
HE DID THE SAME
A DYING CREATURE
WRETCHED FIGURE
HE WAS
WITH LAST WORDS ASKED
OH SAINTLY LEADER
HOW DID I ANGER YOU SO
WITH
TRUMPETS BLOWING
ROCKETS
BURSTING IN AIR
WITH VOICE
LOUDER THAN LOUD
'TIS
JUSTICE AND HONOR
I SWEAR

MY WIFE AND CHILDREN

OFTEN
OFTEN I HAVE TRIED
TO TELL
THE WORLD OF MY LOVE
FOR
JANIS MY WIFE
SCOTT MY SON
REBEKA STEFANIE MY DAUGHTERS
OFTEN
OFTEN WITHOUT SUCCESS
SO IT WILL REMAIN
A SECRET BETWEEN
I
AND
MY CREATOR

SUNSET

WEST
WEST OF
REDS
YELLOWS
MAGENTAS
VIOLETS
MANY
MAJESTIC
POWERFUL
MYSTERIOUS
RAYS
RAYS OF LIGHT
AS I
FACE
THE NORTH STAR

LITTLE SALLY

LITTLE CREATURE
YES YOU ARE
LYING THERE
NOT SO FAR
INNOCENT OF ANY SIN
MOST BEAUTIFUL
YES BY FAR
A SIGH A SIGH
A CRY A CRY
TEARS
ARE ROLLING
FROM YOUR EYES
YOUNG AND INNOCENT
YOUR PAIN IS HERE TO STAY
FATHER MOTHER
EACH WENT A SEPARATE WAY
NOW IT IS YOU
WHO HAS TO PAY

OUT THE WINDOW

I LOOKED
OUT
THE WINDOW
LOOKING
FOR PEACE
SAW WAR
I CRIED

SEARCH

IN SEARCH OF AN ANSWER
I KNOCKED ON A DOOR
LIFE
GAVE ME THE ANSWER
AS I LAID ON THE FLOOR
SUN SHINES TODAY
TOMORROW IT MAY RAIN
TODAY YOU ARE IN HEALTH
TOMORROW IN PAIN
LOOK NOT
PASS YOURSELF WHEN TRYING
TO PLACE THE BLAME
ALONE
WITH MY ANSWER
I LOOKED
WITH MY EYES CLOSED
AND
ALL I SAW WERE LIES

THANKS

I LIKE TO THANK
MY WIFE
FOR HER TRUST
FOR
HER LOVE
I LIKE TO THANK
MY CHILDREN
FOR THEIR LOVE
THEY
WILL NOT BE
DISAPPOINTED

THE CANVAS

AH
IT IS SIMPLE
TO SAY WORDS
WITH LITTLE MEANING
EMPTY SHALLOW WORDS
HAVE KEPT HUMANITY
IN A CONSTANT STATE OF WAR
IF
LIFE WAS A PAINTING
WORDS THE PAINT
AND
I
THE PAINTER
I THROW
AWAY THE PAINT

THE BIRTHDAY

LOOK
THROUGH THE WINDOW
OUT PAST THE RAIN
YOU SEE
A YOUNG MAN
YOU WONDER HIS NAME
A FACE SO LIFELESS
A SMILE SO SAD
SEE HIS TEARS FALLING
MIXING
SLOWLY WITH THE RAIN
ALL THE LIES
ALL THE HORRORS
MUST BE
DRIVING HIM INSANE
LOOK AT THE CALENDAR
LOOK PAST THE WALL
SEE HIS DREAMS CRUMBLE
SEE HIS HOPES FALL
EYES
SLOWLY BURNING
HIS MASK FALLS AWAY
YOU STAND IN HORROR
WONDERING
WHAT IS IT
ALL ABOUT

BODIES

FEAR THEE NOT
SUN MOON AND STARS
FEAR THEE NOT
THE FORCE
SCORCHING THE UNIVERSE
'TIS ONLY
THE SHRILL
CRY OF JOY
WHEN TWO BODIES
HAVE COME TOGETHER
TWO MINDS
TWO MINDS ALIKE
SIMILAR
IN THOUGHT AND DESIRE
TWO BODIES
TWO BODIES
INTERLOCKED

SAD

SAD
BUT TRUE
I THOUGHT MYSELF
AN
OAK TREE
OTHERS KNOW ME
AS
A THORN BUSH

CRY

I WOULD LIKE TO CRY
IF I COULD
I WOULD CRY FOR THE WORLD
YES I WOULD
I WOULD LIKE TO PRAY
IF I COULD
I WOULD PRAY FOR MOTHER NATURE
YES I WOULD
I WOULD LIKE TO SMILE
IF I COULD
I WOULD SMILE FOR YOU
YES I WOULD
I WOULD LIKE TO MAKE THIS EARTH
A PLACE OF PEACE
IF I COULD
FIRST THING I WOULD DO
I DESTROY HUMANITY
YES I WOULD

THE SUN

SUN
QUIT
TRYING TO DECEIVE ME
YOUR
BRIGHT RAYS OF HOPE
SO COMICALLY
DISGUISES
THE DARK PAINT
OF TOMORROW
LIKE THE DESERT
RAIN
YOU
GIVE RELIEF FOR
A FEW MOMENTS
ONLY
TO PROLONG THE AGONY
OF THE LOST
WONDERS
THE BRIGHT FACE
OF THE PROSTITUTE
LIKE THE WORM
ON A FISHING POLE
SERVING A PURPOSE
FOR THE MASTER
THAT BASTARD
SUN
QUIT
TRYING TO DECEIVE
ME
THERE IS LITTLE
HOPE
AS
THE DARK OF DEATH
COMES
OVER MY EYES

YOURSELF

BE YOURSELF
LET YOUR THOUGHTS
FLOW FREE
EXPRESS YOURSELF
LET THE WORLD BE
I HEAR
MANY VOICES
CLAIMING TO BE FREE
BLINDED
BY THE WRONGS THEY HAVE
SEEN
HAVE COMPROMISED
LIFE

UNTITLED

IN YOUR YOUNGER
YEARS WHEN
I TOOK LOVE OF YOU
I BOUGHT YOUR FOOD
I TOLD YOU WHAT TO DO
NOW
YOU ARE GROWN
LIFE IS YOUR OWN
I MUST STAND ASIDE
WATCH YOU WALK
ALONE
MY SON
I'LL WORRY NOT
OF THE THINGS YOU SAY
NOR
OF THE THINGS YOU DO
FOR THE FEW YEARS
I HAD YOU
I
MUST BE GLAD

COLD DAY

COLD WINDY TYPE
DAY
RAINING
EARLY SEPTEMBER
IN TEXAS
DOWN BELOW
MY WINDOW
THE WORLD WILL NOT
STOP
MANY ARE BORN
OTHERS
THEY DIE
I
SIT HERE
ALONE
ON A
COLD WINDY TYPE
DAY

TODAY

TODAY
IS ONE OF THE DARKEST
DAY OF MY LIFE
I WILL SURVIVE
SCATTER
ALL MY FRIENDS
OVER
THE FACE OF THE WORLD
AS
A PEACE OFFERING
TO YOU

WORDS

THINK A LITTLE
BEFORE
YOU SAY WORDS
WHICH
LATER YOU MAY
REGRET
IT IS FUN
TO PASS TIME AWAY
TALKING
ABOUT OLD TIMES
DEAD SKELETONS
ARE BEST KEPT
BURIED
A CARELESS WORD
A CARELESS PHRASE
MAY SOMETIME
HUNT YOU
ONCE DONE
NO MATTER
WHAT
THE WRONG
REMAINS BETTER
IF LEFT UNSAID

UNTITLED

MY SINS
WHY
MUST I CARRY
ALL MY SINS
WRAPPED IN CELLOPHANE
WHY MUST
ALL
SEE
WHAT I'VE BEEN
WHAT I AM
QUESTIONS
LEFT AND FORGOTTEN
BY THAT GREAT
HEALER
CALLED TIME
IF I COULD RELIVE
MY LIFE
THERE
WOULD BE
CHANGES
I WOULD CHOOSE
A MORE SIMPLE
LIFE
YOU FOOL
YOU FOOL
WHY
WORRY ABOUT YESTERDAY
JUST BECAUSE THE
SUN
DID NOT SHINE
TODAY

CRYING

I HAVE TRIED
TO CRY
I CANNOT
THIS DEVIL
WITHIN ME WILL NOT
BE LET OUT
BY TEARS
IT WILL BE DRIVEN
AWAY
WITH HARD WORK
AND
A DESIRE
TO SURVIVE

TRY TRY

I HAVE TRIED TO SMILE
IN A WORLD LIKE TODAY
YOU CAN ONLY TRY
I HAVE TRIED TO DREAM
IN A WORLD LIKE TODAY
YOU CAN ONLY TRY
I HAVE TRIED TO LOVE
IN A WORLD LIKE TODAY
YOU CAN ONLY TRY
I HAVE TRIED TO LIVE IN PEACE
IN A WORLD LIKE TODAY
YOU CAN ONLY TRY

DAYDREAM

LISTEN
TO THE WATER
FLOWING IN THE CREEK
SMELL
MOTHER NATURE
FEEL HER IN YOUR SKIN
LOOK AT THE BIRDS
FLYING
HIGH IN THE SKY
STAND STILL
WHILE THE SNAKE
CREEPS CLOSELY BY
WILD WILD COLORS
MOTHER'S NATURE OWN
I WONDER
MAYBE
IT'S ALL A DREAM
ME AND MY CREATOR
SHARING TOTAL LOVE
JOYOUS LEAPS
WITHIN MY HEART
NOT WARNED
THE TRANCE
IS
BROKEN
BY AN AIRPLANE
FLYING HIGH
ABOVE

LIFE

WE SHOULD NOT
TAKE LIFE SERIOUS
TODAY'S HEROES
ARE TOMORROW'S
FADING MEMORIES
TODAY'S PROBLEMS
ARE TOMORROW'S
PUNCH LINES
WALKING
LIVING FLESH OF TODAY
IS
THE ROTTING DEAD
FLESH OF TOMORROW
THE UNIVERSE
EXIST
WILL EXIST
TOMORROW
DAY AFTER TOMORROW
PHILOSOPHIES
CLASHING TODAY
ARE
TOMORROW'S BED PARTNERS
I SAID IT ONCE
I'LL SAY IT AGAIN
LIFE
IS AN EMPTY CAN
OF BEER

ALONE

I WALK ALONE
HOPING TO FIND A HOME
IF BY CHANCE YOU SEE
A LONELY BOAT OUT AT SEA
REMEMBER
IT'S ONLY ME

© copyright 2010 Jesse Carreon

SICKNESS

DOPE
PROSTITUTION
DRUNKENNESS
OVERWEIGHT
MENTAL ILLNESS
DIVORCE
SIGNS OF A SOCIETY
IN DISTRESS

© copyright 2010 Jesse Carreon

SHED A TEAR

SHED A TEAR
WHEN HE PASSES BY
HE WAS A HERO
HE HAD TO DIE
HE WAS A HERO
TO THE YOUNGER SET
DROVE AROUND
IN A BLUE CORVETTE
TIL
HE WENT A BIT TOO FAST
NOW
HE IS LAID
TO REST

NIGHT

IN THE DARK OF NIGHT
WHEN
THERE IS LITTLE LIGHT
I WILL
HOLD YOU TIGHT
    MY LOVE
    WILL SHINE BRIGHT
IN THE MORNING
WHEN
THE SUN SHINES
I WILL
KNOW YOUR LOVE
IS MINE

NIGHT TIME GIRL

YOU ARE A NIGHT TIME
GIRL
WALKING PAST THE LIGHT
YOUR
NEXT RIDE AWAITS
THERE ON THE SIDE
IT WAS
NOT LONG AGO
YOU LIVED IN A WORLD FAR AWAY
NOW YOU WORK AND SWEAT
DEEP INSIDE
YOU KNOW
EACH RIDE MAKES YOU LESS
PRIDE AND ANGER
YOU MUST ADMIT
A HUNGER
WHICH
MUST BE FED

WEDNESDAY

IT WAS WEDNESDAY
A WEEK AGO
TODAY
WHEN YOU TOLD ME
I MUST GO
WEDNESDAY MORNING
THE SUN WAS BRIGHT
MY HEART WAS
BROKEN
WEDNESDAY NIGHT
IT WAS
SEVEN DAYS AGO
TODAY
WHEN THE PRICE I HAD
TO PAY
A TEAR FELL FROM MY EYE
AS I WALKED
AND PASSED YOU BY

3804 HARLINGEN

MAGIC PLACE OF YESTERYEAR
MUD FIGHTS ROCK FIGHTS
BROTHER AND SISTER FIGHTS
COLD WINTER MORNINGS
BROTHERS SHARING BEDS
GOOD EATING
A GARDEN IN OUR BACK YARD
MOTHER'S FLOWERS
THE GARAGE MY DAD BUILT
SUNDAY MORNINGS
BIRTHDAY PARTIES
CHRISTMAS PARTIES
WRESTLING MATCHES
AND
MUCH MORE
MAGIC PLACE OF YESTERYEAR
HOME
MY CHILDHOOD HOME

© copyright 2010 Jesse Carreon

DEATH

DEATH MY FRIEND
COME HELP ME END
END
THAT WHICH NEVER BEGAN
MISTAKEN
SOMEONE MUST HAVE BEEN
TOMORROW
AN INFINITY AWAY
YESTERDAY WAS THE SAME
I SEE
NO FURTHER THAN TODAY
I LIVE WITHOUT
MEMORIES NOR HOPE

STREET PERSON

WALKING
DEEP IN CONTEMPLATION
LATE
THE QUIETNESS OF THE STREET
THE FAR AWAY SOUND
OF A TRUCK ON THE FREEWAY
WOULD NOT LET ME FORGET
IT'S LATE LATE NIGHT
OR
EARLY EARLY MORNING
IT MAY HAVE BEEN
MY IMAGINATION
I WAS CALLED
OUT OF MY CONTEMPLATION
THEREUPON
HE APPROACH ME
A STRANGER
I SENSED DANGER
HIS FACE FULL OF PAIN
IN HIS EYES SO MUCH SORROW
I ASKED
IF I COULD HELP
HE SMILED
I UNDERSTOOD
A STRANGER
I TRIED TO HELP
I HAD
NOT ASKED HIS NAME
AS I TURNED
TO WALK AWAY
I
NOTICED IT WAS
RAINING

BAD NEWS FOR MRS. BROWN

TUESDAY MORNING
SUN SHINING BRIGHT
MRS. BROWN OPENED THE DOOR
OUTSIDE
WESTERN UNION CAME
SORRY
I GOT BAD NEWS TODAY
YOUR ONLY SON
WAS LAST SEEN
FIGHTING ALONE
LIKE A GOOD MARINE
LATER
A MAN CAME
SAYING
HIS DEATH WAS A CRYING SHAME
10,000.00 DOLLARS
AND A PURPLE HEART
THAT WAS TWO YEARS AGO
TODAY
NO ONE SEES HER DAILY TRIPS
TO A COLD STONE LAYING FLAT
ON THE GROUND

© copyright 2010 Jesse Carreon

DYING MAN

I STOOD
WATCHED A MAN DIE
CAN'T SAY
I THINK HE CRIED
A TEAR COMING FROM HIS EYE
DON'T CRY SAID I
YOU'LL BE MUCH BETTER DEAD
IF BY CHANCE
SOME LATER DAY
I HAPPEN TO WALK
PASSED YOUR WAY
REMEMBER
IT WAS I
WHO STOOD BY YOUR SIDE
WATCHED YOU DIE

CASUALTY

MY INSIDES ARE TORN ASUNDER
SCATTERED
AMONG THE GRASS AND DIRT
MY MIND REFUSES TO FUNCTION
MY WHOLE LIFE
RUSHES BEFORE MY EYES
IN TOMORROW'S NEWSPAPER
HALFWAY
AROUND THE WORLD
I WILL BECOME A NUMBER
ANOTHER CASUALTY
NO NAME
NO FACE
NO FEELINGS
THE POLITICIANS ARGUING
THE JUST CAUSE FOR WAR
THE PREACHERS
JUSTIFYING NATIONAL INTEREST
THE PEOPLE
BEING LED LIKE COWS
AND
I
I DON'T COUNT
SOON
I WILL BE DEAD
A CASUALTY

© copyright 2010 Jesse Carreon

MY CHILDREN

I CAN HEAR THE THUMP
ON THE CARPET FLOOR
THE SHUFFLING OF FEET
2, 4, 6
THUMP THUMP THUMP
HI DADDY HI DADDY
THIS IS HOW I AWAKE
EACH MORNING
NO MATTER THE PROBLEMS
NO MATTER THE PAIN
IT ALL DISAPPEARS
BLOWN AWAY
REPLACED BY
THREE SMILING FACES
OH LORD
IF MY DAY
COULD
BE COMPRESSED
INTO
THESE FEW MINUTES

PEACE

PEACE
TO MEN OF GOOD WILL
PEACE
PEACE
MAY
THERE COME A DAY
WHEN
WE ALL CAN SAY
PEACE
PEACE
FOR
THE WORLD TODAY
LET US NOT FORGET
TO SAY
PEACE
PEACE

THE SKY

THE SKY
MAN
ANIMAL
ALL
ALL MAKE UP THE WORLD
HATE
ENVY
DECEIT
INJUSTICE
ALL
ALL MAKE UP THE WORLD
LOVE
JUSTICE
PEACE
HONOR
ALL
ALL MAKE UP THE WORLD

HONOR MY FRIEND

I KNOW OF A MAN
OUT OF WORK
HUNGRY
HIS FAMILY HUNGRY
HIS SOUL
TORN BETWEEN
RIGHT AND WRONG
I KNOW OF A MAN IN NEED
RETURNED A BILLFOLD
FOUND FULL OF MONEY
TO THE POLICE

GETTING OLD

I AM NOT GETTING
YOUNGER
LIFE IS FAST GOING
PAST MY WAY
I SIT
I KNOW NOT WHAT TO SAY
NOT
LONG AGO I WAS A YOUNG BOY
PLAYING
WITH MY BRAND NEW TOY
A SHORT SLEEP AND I AWAKE
TO FIND
I AM NOT A BOY
YESTERDAY
I WAITED FOR MOM TO CALL
'DINNER READY'
TODAY
I WAIT
NOT FOR MOTHER
RATHER I GO
TO MY WIFE AND CHILD
TODAY
MOTHER AND DAD
ARE NOT SO YOUNG
NOR SEEM AS TALL
TODAY
MY LIFE
IS FAST COMING TO AN END
BACK
TO WHERE
IT ALL BEGAN

© copyright 2010 Jesse Carreon

YOUNG MAN

A YOUNG MAN
ABOUT TO DIE
LAYING IN MUD
DIRTY BOOTS
TORN SHIRT
A BULLET
THROUGH HIS HEAD
RED DROPS FALLING
PAST
HIS SUNKEN WORRIED EYES
IF HE COULD HE WOULD ASK
WHY
IN RETURN A MEDAL
SOON TO BE FORGOTTEN
OH
THAT'S NOT ALL
A 3X6 IN ARLINGTON
TOO
WARM SUN SHINING BRIGHT
HE
WILL BE WITH YOU
TONIGHT
YOUNG MAN ABOUT TO DIE
IF
WE KNEW THE REASON
WHY
IF WE KNEW

MAN

MEN LIKE FLOWERS
WILL WITHER AND DIE
TIME WILL ERASE
ALL SCARS
FROM HIS FACE
HE WILL BE RETURNED
TO WHAT HE IS
DIRT

CRYING MAN

I THOUGHT
I SAW A YOUNG MAN CRYING
NO
HE IS ONLY DYING
YOUNG HERO
A PAWN
NOTHING MORE
PRIDE MISUNDERSTANDING
ASK A HIGH PRICE
FROM MAN
I THOUGHT
I SAW A YOUNG MAN CRYING
NO
HE IS ONLY DYING
POLITICAL MISTAKES
AWASHED IN BLOOD
THE RIPPLE
BECOMES A FLOOD
PEACE
A FALSE ILLUSION
HATE HAS CLOGGED
THE CHANNELS OF OUR MIND

DARK ROOM

DARKENED ROOM
TWO LOVERS
EXPLORING
TREMBLING FINGERS
QUIVERING LIPS
CRIES OF JOY
EAGER FOR
THE MOMENT

DAYTIME

ON THE BETTER
SIDE OF DAY
THE SUN SHINES
THE BIRDS SING
YOU
ARE HERE WITH
ME

GRAVE

WHEN MY BODY
IN ITS GRAVE DOES LIE
AND
MY SOUL WITH TIME
DOES FLY
IT WILL BE TIME
FOR THE WORM TO COME
ONE AT FIRST
BUT THERE'LL BE MORE
SLOWLY
THEY WILL EAT ME BACK
TO DIRT
RETURNED
BACK TO MOTHER EARTH
NINE MONTHS FOR ME TO
BE
NOW HERE I LIE
    DOWN IN THE GROUND
THE WORMS
ARE ALL AROUND
BE GENTLE
YOU DIRTY CREATURES
TRY NOT TO DISGRACE
MY LOVELY FEATURES
I'LL LIVE
TRY NOT TO BE A CLOWN
REMEMBERING
WHAT AWAITS ME
DOWN IN THE GROUND

DEATH

DEATH
I WILL LOOK YOU
IN THE EYE
I WILL NOT ASK
WHY
MY DAYS ARE NUMBERED
I KNOW
I WON'T BE AFRAID
TO GO
I'LL NOT CRY
I'LL NOT FRET
I WILL ACCEPT
DEATH
YOU
I WILL NOT AWAIT
NOR
WILL I FORGET
ON A GIVEN DAY
YOU AND I
WILL WALK
HAND IN HAND
I CANNOT
NOT SAY I HATE TO GO
LIFE FOREVER
IS NOT MY
GOAL

© copyright 2010 Jesse Carreon

BLIND EYES

I NEED
NOT SEE THE STARS
I NEED
NOT SEE THE ATOM
I NEED
NOT SEE A THOUGHT
I NEED
NOT SEE MY SOUL
I KNOW
THEY EXIST
LIKEWISE
MY LOVE FOR YOU

BIRTH

WAS IT NOT
A SHORT TIME
AGO
MY BIRTH
SO SOON
MY LIFE
PASSED
EVEN NOW
I SEE
DEAD I AM NOT
MY MARK
ON EARTH
HAS BEGUN
TO FADE
SOON
TO BE FORGOTTEN

SALLY MCCRACKLING

A GIRL
CALLED
SALLY MCCRACKLING
KINDA TALL
NOT GOOD LOOKING
IN THE KITCHEN
SHE
WAS ALWAYS COOKING
BILLY
HER BOY
SHE WAS
TRYING TO HOOK HIM
CAME A DAY
THE 13 OF DECEMBER
ONE AND ALL
CAN STILL REMEMBER
IN A BEER JOINT
DOWN IN TOWN
BILLY HIMSELF
GOT SHOT DOWN
CRAZY MARY
WHO
LIVED DOWN THE ALLEY
WENT THROUGH TOWN
SHOUTING FOR SALLY

HURRY GIRL
COME DOWN TO THE
'PRAIRIE'
THERE
BILLY BOY
WAS SHOUTING
FOR SALLY
DYING BILLY HELD
ON TO SALLY
WHILE THE PREACHER
RAN THROUGH
THE ALLEY

MY DOG

I ASKED MY DOG
IF HE COULD SEE
HE ANSWERED
YES
I ASKED MY DOG
IF HE COULD SMELL
HE ANSWERED
YES
I ASKED MY DOG
IF HE COULD FEEL
HE ANSWERED
YES
I ASKED MY DOG
IF HE COULD LOVE
HE GAVE HIS LIFE
FOR MINE

MY WIFE'S MOTHER

IT IS WELL
UNDERSTOOD
YOU THINK
I AM NO GOOD
YOUR ONLY CHILD
YOU LIKE TO SEE
MARRY
SOMEONE OTHER THAN
ME
LOVE
IS ALL I GOT TO GIVE
A FEW PROMISES I WISH TO KEEP
EVERYTHING ELSE
LIES WITHIN MY HEART
IF SHE WANTS MORE
THEN
I WILL DEPART

MY SON AND DAUGHTERS

A WARNING
IT'S NO BIG DEAL TO MARRY
A HOLY MAN
SAYS A FEW WORDS
A CITY OFFICIAL
STAMPS A CHEAP
PIECE OF PAPER
IT'S NO BIG DEAL
TO BECOME
A FATHER OR MOTHER
A FEW MOMENTS
OF RAW PLEASURE
THE SEED
IS PLANTED
TO BE A PARENT
IT IS EASIER TO CATCH
THE WIND
IT IS EASIER TO OUTRUN
THE SUN

SIN

LIKE THE POPE
WHEN YOU ARE TOO OLD
TO SIN
MIGHT AS WELL
BE
AGAINST IT

ALABAMA

(Watching tv in the 60's)
DON'T CRY MY FRIEND
THE COUNTRY
BELONGS TO YOU
TOO
LIKE THE ANIMALS
AT THE ZOO
THEY HAVE ASSIGNED
A PLACE FOR YOU
GRATEFUL
YOU SHOULD BE
THERE IS EQUALITY
AS
YOU CAN SEE
WORK HARD
KNOW YOUR PLACE
HARD WORKING
'BOYS'
I APPRECIATE
SWEAT SWEAT SWEAT
DRIP DRIP DRIP
GOOD
FOR YOUR COUNTRY
DON'T GET THE
BIG HEAD

MISSING THE BOAT

YOU CAN SEE THEM
EVERY SUNDAY
THE MORNING
WHEN THEY COME TO PRAY
ONE HOUR
EVERY SUNDAY
PRESSED SUITS
NEW DRESSES
FLASHY NEW CARS
BRIGHT FACES
GOOD INTENTIONS
HOPE
LOVE
UNDERSTANDING
IN BIG AND FANCY
CHURCHES
WITH
TRUE CONTRITION
THEY COME TO PRAY
GOD'S
LOVE AND UNDERSTANDING
FROM THE PULPIT
THEY HEAR THE PREACHER
SAY
ONE HOUR
EVERY SUNDAY
HATE
IS GONE AWAY

ONE HOUR
EVERY SUNDAY
WITH THE DOLLAR
THEY BUY THEIR WAY
PEACE OF MIND
A TRUE ILLUSION
AND
A DOLLAR IS ALL THEY
PAY

NO WORDS

MY JANIS MY WIFE
THROW AWAY ALL WORDS
SAY
SHE IS MY 'MONA LISA'
SAY
SHE IS MY 'SISTINE CHAPEL'
MY MIRACLE
I LOVE HER

ME

MANY TIMES
I HAVE
DONE WRONG
MORE THAN ONCE
I CRIED
LATE INTO THE NIGHT
LIFE
A STUMBLING
BLOCK
NO ONE BUT I
CAN SEE THROUGH
MY EYES
IN THE MORNING
WHEN I AWAKE
AGAIN
I WILL FACE
THE DAY

THE WORD

MANY YEARS AGO
ON A MOUNTAIN
A MAN WE ALL KNOW
THERE
HE GOT THE WORD
TEN ALL TOGETHER
IMPORTANT ONLY TWO
LOVE GOD
FRIENDS AND NEIGHBORS
ENEMIES TOO
WISE WORDS
WE ARE TOLD
SACRED SO WE SAY
WE LOVE
GOD
OUR NEIGHBOR
HELP OUR FRIENDS
MOST IMPORTANT
WE BOMB
OUR ENEMIES
LIKE THE WORD
TOLD US TO

OFTEN

I AIN'T UNDERSTOOD
BY THOSE
I LOVE
HOW CAN THEY
WHEN
I KNOW
LITTLE OF MYSELF
OR
MY id

FINISHED

JUST LIKE NAPOLEON
YOUR
DAYS ARE THROUGH
IN
THE DARK OF NIGHT
THE CAT COMES FOR YOU
DARK GREEN EYES
LOOKING
FOR HIS FAVORITE CLOWN
HE LOOKS FOR NONE
BUT YOU
THE NIGHT WIND CALLS YOUR NAME
YOU SAY YOU ARE NOT
HE KNOWS THE TRUTH
NOTHING MUCH YOU CAN DO
IN DARK CORNERS YOU FOUND
YOUR THRILLS
ON STREET CORNERS YOU EARN
YOUR BILL
TIME NOW
TO PAY FOR YOUR CHEAP THRILLS
INSTANT DERIVATIVES OF HAPPINESS
YOU CANNOT FIND
STOP TRYING
TO BLOW YOUR MIND
LOOKING
OUT FROM WITHIN
OH WHAT'S THE USE
THE TIME
HAS COME TO PAY YOUR
DUES

SILENCE

SILENCE WHERE ARE YOU
WITHIN A HOLE
DOWN IN THE GROUND
LAYING FACE DOWN
MORTALLY WOUNDED
I HAVE BEEN
BY
ALL THE NOISE ABOVE
SO HERE I'LL LAY
TILL THE END OF TIME
GOODBYE
OH MY
DON'T CRY

LAUGH

THE SUN IS SHINING
THE SKY IS BLUE
YESTERDAY
DREAMS ARE COMING TRUE
BIRDS ARE SINGING
BELLS ARE RINGING
MY HEART MY LOVE
I GIVE TO YOU
THE MOON IS FULL
THE SKY IS CLEAR
YOUR LOVE YOUR TOUCH
I WANT NEAR
SAD DAYS
BLUE NIGHTS
HAVE GONE AWAY
YOUR LOVE MY SUN
YOUR HEART MY JOY

OH GOD

(a conversation with GOD in a moment of despair)
GOD
I'LL
NOT TRUST YOU
BELIEVE IN YOU
JUSTICE
HA
YOUR CHURCH
ON EARTH
TELL ME
ANOTHER JOKE
YOUR LOVE
MEN'S LOVE
YOUR TEACHINGS
A FORM
OF SERVITUDE
ONE MAN
KNELT BEFORE ANOTHER
HEAVEN
CAN BE BOUGHT

UNTITLED

DON'T
CALL MY NAME
SAY GOODBYE
WALK AWAY
I WILL LIVE

THE EVOLUTION CAKE

WHEN
AND IF I COULD
WILLED
AND
ALL WOULD BE MISUNDERSTOOD
TAKE SIMPLICITY
BAKE
A COMPLICATED CAKE
PLACING IT UPON
THE GROUND
SIT WAIT
FOR MAN
TO BE BORN

BAD DREAM

I AWOKE
HAD A
BAD DREAM
THAT DARK PIT
MY BODY FLOATING
AS IF BY MAGIC
DEEPER DEEPER
HELP HELP
I CRIED
TWICE MAYBE MORE
FROM HIGH ABOVE
I HEARD A VOICE
I THINK
IT MAY HAVE BEEN
CHRIST
'SORRY YOU HAD YOUR CHANCE'

SHELL

MORE THAN A BODY
SOMEONE WITHIN ME
THERE HAS TO BE
OTHERWISE
THERE WOULD BE NO YOU
OR ME

THE TRINITY

1+2=3
2+1=3
1+1+1=3
3+0=3
INFINITY=3
I AM

MAY I

MAY I DREAM
MAY I HOPE
MAY I LOVE
YES
YOU MAY DREAM
YES
YOU MAY HOPE
YES
YOU MAY LOVE
REMEMBER
INFINITY
DOES
HAVE AN END

THIS WORLD

IN THIS WORLD
I SIT
SURROUNDED BY NAUGHT
IN MY LONELINESS
I CRY
I HAVE SEEN
THE WORLD
I HAVE RETURNED HOME
NO MORE TO LEAVE

GOING TO CHURCH

ON A CLEAR SUNDAY MORNING
WITH BOB DYLAN
SINGING THE BLUES
ALL MY CHILDREN RUNNING LOOSE
MY WIFE
IN THE BATHROOM
I
I SIT
I SIT WONDERING
IF 300% 400%
PROFITS
CLAIMED BY THE OIL
KINGS
IS ENOUGH TO BUY ST. PETER
IN A FEW MOMENTS
OFF TO CHURCH I GO
WITH HUMILITY
ON BENT KNEES
I WILL ASK FORGIVENESS
FOR MY SINS
AND FOR HELP
TO MAKE IT THROUGH
ANOTHER DAY
AS
A PARTING FAVOR
MAYBE
JUST MAYBE
I
COULD BE HAPPY
WITH THE PROBLEMS FACED
BY
EXXON MOBIL AND SHELL

MY WIFE AND KIDS

I
SOMETIMES WONDER
WHAT
GIVES ME STRENGTH
TO FACE
ANOTHER DAY
WITH
THANKS AND HUMILITY
I ANSWER
MY WIFE AND KIDS

© copyright 2010 Jesse Carreon

ANGRY

THEY
HAVE SCREWED MOTHER NATURE
THEY
HAVE BLED HER DRY
NOW
IN ANGER SHE AWAKES
TO
DEAL HUMANITY
A
DESERVING BLOW

© copyright 2010 Jesse Carreon

WORD

IF MY WORD
WOULD BE ALL I NEED
FOR ME
TO HAVE MY WAY
A WOMAN
I WOULD CALL
TAKE HER HOME WITH ME

© copyright 2010 Jesse Carreon

FOR JANIS

YOU ARE TO ME
WHAT A DOCK IS TO A SHIP
I MAY ROAM IN THIS SEA
CALLED LIFE
FROM
PORT TO PORT
LOST AND CONFUSED
I KNOW
I HAVE A PLACE
CALLED HOME
ONLY YOU
MAKE LIFE WORTH
LIVING

© copyright 2010 Jesse Carreon

BAD DAY

TODAY
IS A BAD DAY FOR A FUNERAL
THE SUN IS SHINING
THE SKY IS BLUE
IT IS NOT
A GOOD DAY FOR A FUNERAL
YESTERDAY
WAS A GOOD DAY FOR A FUNERAL
THE SUN DIDN'T SHINE
THE SKY WAS DARK
YESTERDAY
WAS A GOOD DAY FOR A FUNERAL
I'D LIKE FOR THE SUN TO SHINE
ON MY DAY TO BE BURIED

BAD LUCK

THE SUN DON'T SHINE NO MORE
MY CAR WON'T START
MY GIRL IS ON HER PERIOD
MY LAST CHECK WILL BOUNCE
ONCE OR TWICE
THOSE ARABS ARE FORCING
FUEL PRICES UP
IT DON'T MATTER
CAUSE I'M GETTING
DRUNK

WHISPERS

AH
YOU HAVE WHISPERED
SWEET WORDS IN MY EAR
YOUR LIPS
SWEET AS SWEET CAN BE
WE ARE
DIFFERENT AS NIGHT TO DAY
I AM
A PART OF A GAME YOU PLAY

FOR JANIS

WE
IN OUR OWN WAY
WILL SHARE LIFE
GIVING AND TAKING
SMILE
WHEN IT IS TIME TO SMILE
CRY
WHEN IT IS TIME TO CRY
SO IT WILL BE
TILL ONE OF US DIES
THEN WE WILL SAY
GOODBYE

VISIT

THE SUN GOES UP
THE SUN COMES DOWN
THE WORLD
KEEPS TURNING 'ROUND
THE NIGHT COMES
THEN IT IS GONE
THE FLOWERS
CONTINUE TO BLOOM
YOU
ARE ON MY MIND
IN THE EARLY HOURS
BEFORE
THE BREAK OF DAWN
I
BRING YOU PRETTY FLOWERS
FRESH
AS THE NEW DAY'S DAWN
YOU LEFT EARLY
YOU GAVE NO WARNING
NOW I LEAVE THE CEMETERY
I WISH
I TOO
WAS DEAD

FOREVER

DAY AFTER TOMORROW
WHEN
MOST OF OUR PAINS AND SORROWS
ARE A MEMORY
WHEN
OUR DREAMS ARE LESS EXCITING
WHEN
EVENING BRINGS EXCITING
TALES OF EARLY YEARS
WHEN
DEATH'S DOOR IS A STEP CLOSER
DAY AFTER TOMORROW
WHEN
THE YOUNG ARE FULL GROWN
WHEN
THE OLD IS A MEMORY
WHEN
THE NEW CAR IS A WRECK
WHEN
THE NEW HOUSE SHOWS ITS AGE
DAY AFTER TOMORROW
WHEN
NEW DREAMS HAVE MADE OURS
OLD
I WILL
STILL LOVE YOU

© copyright 2010 Jesse Carreon

HURT

MY TOMORROW
WILL NOT BE THE SAME
YOU
MY LOVE
WILL BE TO BLAME
CARELESS WORDS
WERE NEVER MEANT
TO BE
YOU SPOKE
WORDS MEANT
FOR SOMEONE ELSE
NOT ME

FUNNY BODIES

LOOK
AT THE FUNNY BODIES
THE ONES
WITH THE PAINTED FACE
I HEARD SOMEPLACE
I DON'T KNOW WHERE
THEY ARE CALLED THE HUMAN RACE
RUNNING
SHOUTING
LAUGHING
NOT KNOWING WHERE THEY GO
I KNOW THE SUGAR DADDY
THE ONE
WITH THE MONEY STICK
HE IS
THE ONE WHO MAKES THINGS
TICK
NO WONDER THEY ARE
SICK

UNTITLED

TWO YEARS AWAY FROM THE TEENS
YOU'VE BEEN A WOMAN SINCE 13
THIS MAGIC DAY
HAS BEEN YOUR DREAM
SINCE THE DAY YOU TURNED 19
NOW
IT IS NOT QUITE CLEAR
WHY
YOU HELD THIS DAY SO DEAR

© copyright 2010 Jesse Carreon

TWILIGHT

TWILIGHT OF MY TIME
IS FAST APPROACHING
DIVERGENT ROADS
LONG TRAVELED
MERGING
AT A COMMON INTERSECTION
CHOICES MADE
MUST NOW BE MEASURED AND WEIGHED
A MIXED AROMA
BOTH
SWEET AND NOXIOUS
THE AFTERMATH OF A LONG
LIFE
THE BEAUTY OF SNOW
THE SOUND OF RAIN
IS A MEMORY TREASURED
'TIL WE ARE WEAK AND OLD
WE VIEW THE WORLD
WE SEE IT FALLING
I WONDER IF MEN
IF MAN MUST ALWAYS WALK ALONE

© copyright 2010 Jesse Carreon

OUR PROBLEMS

WE HAD OUR PROBLEMS
TROUBLES WE HAD MORE
THAN OUR SHARE
NO MATTER OUR MISERIES
ALWAYS
REMEMBER I CARE
TO LOSE YOU
I KNOW WOULD HURT
SOMEHOW
I WOULD PULL THROUGH
TO LOSE MY CHILDREN
OH LORD
THAT DAY WOULD
BE MY END

A TREE

IF I COULD HAVE A CHOICE
TO BE
I WOULD TURN
MYSELF INTO A TREE
STANDING THERE
BOTH DAY AND NIGHT
WITHIN MY ARMS
CHILDREN
WOULD PLAY
TILL
THE END OF DAY

REMEMBRANCE

AN AFTERNOON AT THE LAKE
AT FIRST GLANCE
IT IS SO DECEIVING
SO PEACEFUL AND SERENE
MAKES
YOU WONDER IF IT IS NOT ALL A DREAM
MAN AND NATURE IN HARMONY
SENDS YOUR SPIRIT SOARING
HIGH AND FREE
THE SUN RAYS WARM REFLECTION
SENDS YOUR MIND IN RECOLLECTION
OF THE DAY
NOT LONG AGO
WHEN
THE CRY OF ALL NATIONS
WAS
PREPARE YOURSELF FOR
WAR

© copyright 2010 Jesse Carreon

VIRGIN

A VIRGIN YOU SHOULD BE
FOR THE PLEASURES
YOU HAVE GIVEN ME
AH
WOMAN
HOW YOU DECEIVED
WITH PROMISES
THAT NEVER WERE MEANT
TO BE

© copyright 2010 Jesse Carreon

UNDER THE TREE

WALKING DOWN THE STREET
A FEW
OR
NO ONE ELSE IN SIGHT
STARS SHINING BRIGHT
WHERE COULD MY LOVE BE
LOVELY GIRL
IF YOU COULD BE WITH ME
BENEATH THIS TREE
COOL GRASS OUR BED WOULD BE
NO ONE WOULD TELL
THE FUN WE HAD
INSTEAD
HERE I LAY
BENEATH THIS TREE
ONLY THE ANTS AND ME
BRIGHT MOON ANOTHER
NIGHT HAS PASSED ME BY

LOOK INTO DARKNESS

SEE THERE
SEE THERE
THERE THERE
LIES TRUTH
MORTALLY WOUNDED
SPLIT ASUNDER
BY THE HONOR
OF MANKIND

DEATH BELL

I HEAR
THE DEATH BELL RING
IT'S A SAD SONG IT SINGS
MAN
WOMAN
BOY
GIRL
A FINAL DAWN HAS COME
CARS ARE MOVING
TIME GOES BY
TEARS ARE FALLING
FROM SOMEONE'S EYES
PLEASANT JOURNEY
TO YOU MY FRIEND
HOPE YOU HAD A HAPPY END
THE DEATH BELL RINGS
IT'S A SAD SONG IT SINGS
DOWN DOWN YOU GO
DOWN
INTO THAT DIRTY HOLE
NOW AND FOREVER
TILL THE END OF TIME
NEVER AGAIN
TO
HAVE A GLASS OF WINE

A WISH

GIVE
UNDERSTANDING
HUMANITY
IS LEARNING
TO GET ALONE
TOGETHER
CALLING EACH
BROTHER
LET GO
OF YOUR VANITY
LOVE
YOU GOT TO GIVE
FOR THIS
WORLD
TO BE FREE

NO TOY

DON'T
PLAY GAMES WITH ME
I AM NOT YOURS
IF IT SEEMS
YOU ARE A PART OF ME
YOU ARE
FOR JUST AWHILE
I HAVE
AND
I WILL
LIVE WITHOUT YOU

LOVE YOU

YOU WANT ME TO LOVE YOU
YOU WANT ME TO CARE
YOU KNOW
YOU KNOW
I LOVE YOU
I CARE
FOR NO ONE ELSE
YOU WISH ME TO HELP YOU
HELP WITH THIS LIFE
I WISH THE SAME
I WISH YOU BY MY SIDE
DO NOT
TRY TO CHANGE ME
I
I COULD NEVER BE
I CAN FACE ALL FAILURES
I CAN TAKE ALL THE PAIN
WITH
YOU BY MY SIDE

LAST DAYS

ON
THESE
LAST FEW DAYS
OF LIFE
I WILL
SPEND THEM AS I PLEASE
SAD
GLAD
OR
OTHERWISE
NO MORE
YESTERDAYS
TODAYS
NO
TOMORROWS
BEST
NO MORE
SORROW

MAMA

MAMA
THE LEAVES ARE FALLING
WHAT DOES IT MEAN
TREES ARE SO PRETTY
WHEN
THEY ARE FULL AND GREEN
WHEN THEY LOSE
THEIR DRESSING
THEY LOOK SO MEAN
MAMA
I HEAR A STORM
RUMBLING
ACROSS OUR LAND
MAMA
I CAN'T SEE
DO YOU UNDERSTAND
MAMA
THE LEAVES ARE FALLING

IF

IF YOU WOULD LET ME
I WOULD PAINT THE WORLD
JUST FOR YOU
IF YOU WOULD LET ME
I WOULD DREAM ALL MY DREAMS
JUST FOR YOU
IF YOU WOULD LET ME
I WOULD LAUGH ALL MY LAUGHS
JUST FOR YOU
IF YOU WOULD LET ME
I WOULD GIVE MY LIFE
JUST FOR YOU
IF YOU WOULD LET ME
I WOULD DIE MY DEATH
JUST FOR YOU

GOD BLESS YOU

GOD BLESS YOU
ALL GOOD PEOPLE
THE WAR IS OVER
ONCE AGAIN
FORMER ENEMIES
ARE
NOW SITTING DOWN TO TEA
THE SUN SHINES BRIGHTER
THE WIND OF WAR HAS DIED DOWN
GOD BLESS YOU
ALL GOOD PEOPLE
MAY NONE OF YOU
GO TO HELL
CITIES ARE QUIET
MAY THERE BE PEACE
TIME TO ENJOY LIFE
SMILE TO ALL YOU SEE
GOD BLESS YOU
ALL GOOD PEOPLE
DON'T
HOLD YOUR BREATH

© copyright 2010 Jesse Carreon

MINUTE WITHIN THE HOUR

A MINUTE WITHIN THE HOUR
THE SKY IS DARK
THERE WILL BE SHOWERS
TO
REMIND US ALL OF THE HOUR
THE FLOWER IS DEAD
THE SUN IS DYING
MAN ALONE
AND
HE IS CRYING
FROM
SWEET WINE COMES MISERY
SAID THE FLOWER TO THE VINE
THE ROOM IS DARK THERE IS CONFUSION
NO WONDER
THERE IS SO MUCH DILUTION
THE TIME HAD COME
NOW IT'S GONE
FOR
ALL GOOD MEN TO COME HOME
THE SUN HAS DIED
YOU STAND THERE CRYING
NO USE IN YOU DENYING
A MAN YOU ARE
YOU GOT TO BE
YOU CANNOT CHANGE
INTO A DRIED OLD TREE

HEAVEN'S LIGHT IS NOW SHINING
AIN'T NO USE IN YOU CRYING
FOR
THE RIGHT TO BE MISUNDERSTOOD
DARKNESS COME TO EVERY DAY
NOW
IT'S TIME FOR YOU TO PAY
A MINUTE WITHIN THE HOUR
THE PRICE FOR LIVING
IS NOW
DYING

© copyright 2010 Jesse Carreon

I A FAILURE

I REFUSE
TO BE MACHINED
REWARDED WITH A DIPLOMA
I REFUSE
TO BE MOLDED AND REARRANGED
STAMPED WITH THE SUCCESS LABEL
I REFUSE
TO BELIEVE FOUR YEARS
OF CONCENTRATED STUDIES
WILL MAKE ME A BETTER
MAN
I REFUSE
TO WALK THROUGH A DOOR
OPENED BY A 12 X 14 STATUS SYMBOL
SUCCESS WILL BE MINE
IF I AM MYSELF
I AM A SUCCESS
IF I LIKE WHAT I AM
I DO NOT NEED A DIPLOMA
TO BE COMPLETE
I HAVE MY OWN DREAM

CHRIST

I WOULD LIKE TO
SHARE YOUR PAIN
I WOULD LIKE TO
HELP CARRY YOUR CROSS
MAYBE
I COULD ADJUST
THE CROWN
LESSEN THE PAIN
A BIT
I KNOW IT IS
HARD TO BELIEVE
I AM A MAN
FORGIVE ME

TOTAL LOVE

LOVE CAN BE TOTAL
HATE IS TOTAL
THE WORLD CANNOT
ALLOW ITSELF TO KNOW
THE BEAUTY OF TOTAL LOVE
IF
NOT FOR MISTRUST OR HATE
OUR ECONOMY
WOULD COME TO A STOP
LIKE IT OR NOT
A PERSON'S DEATH
LEAKS OUT ANOTHER DOLLAR
FOR US
THE HUNGRY DOGS

THOUGHTS

(while watching the sun go down)
LOOK AT THE SUNSET
SAD IT HAD TO DIE
NOT LONG AGO
BRIGHT AND POWERFUL
IT
THE CENTER OF THE SKY
NOW
SO SAD IT'S DYING
I WONDER
IF IT CAN RECALL
THE JOY AND SORROWS
IT BROUGHT TO SOME OR ALL
AS I SIT
WATCHING AN EMPIRE FALL
I WONDER IF TOMORROW
IT WILL BE MY TIME
TO GO

SALLY

SMALL
PRETTY AND BROWN
EYES
LARGE AND BROWN

I AM

I AM OR AM I
JUST A DREAM
TO
BE ERASED BY THE RISING
SUN
AM I REAL
A MAN
A god's PASSING FANCY
OR
A GAME HE PLAYS
IF I AM NOT
WHAT I SEE CANNOT EXIST
AM I DREAM
A SCHEME OF A FOOL
AM I OR AM I
A TOY OF A god
HE
WHO SITS HIGH ABOVE
PLAYING
AS IF I WAS A GAME OF
MONOPOLY
SEVEN GIVES ME SEVEN MOVES
SNAKE EYES I GO TO JAIL
OR IS IT HELL
AM I
A QUESTION NOT KNOWN
TO SOME

© copyright 2010 Jesse Carreon

CHANGING TIMES

TIME IS CHANGING
CAN'T SAY THE CHANGE
IS GOOD
I KNOW
IT WILL BE
MISUNDERSTOOD

DAYTIME BLUES

YOU WAKE UP EARLY
TROUBLE IS
YOU LEAVE
YOU LEAVE ME ALONE
I TRIED TO TELL YOU
OUR NEXT DOOR NEIGHBOR
IS LOOKING GOOD
YOU COME TO BED
TROUBLE IS
YOU GO TO SLEEP
I LAY NEXT TO YOU
THAT NEIGHBOR
SURE LOOKS GOOD
SHE TELLS
HER HUSBAND IS GONE
MOST OF THE TIME
AIN'T GOT NO IDEAS
YET
I AM THINKING

NO CHANGE

I AWOKE
AND
EVERYTHING WAS STILL THE SAME
TOOK A WALK THROUGH TOWN
SAW KIDS
LOOKING AROUND KILLING TIME
YOUNG GIRLS
WITH THEIR FIRST MISTAKE
MORNING PAPER
BAD NEWS
WAR AND KILLINGS
WHAT'S THE USE
TEN DEAD THIRTEEN MISSING
THE POPE IS OUT
GIVING BLESSINGS
LITTLE HOPE FOR PEACE IS SEEN
A NEW WAR IS BREWING
I
SIT HERE DRINKING
MY HIGH PRICE JUICE
A SOCIAL DISORDER
MAN
KILLING ONE ANOTHER

CRY

I WOULD CRY
EXCEPT
I RAN OUT OF TEARS
LIFE IS NOT EXACTLY
A BUNDLE OF JOY
I WOULD LIKE TO AWAKE
FIND
A NEW SUN SHINING
I KNOW I WON'T
WHY WASTE
YOUR TIME AND MINE
TELLING YOU
OF MY DREAMS

FREED

WHEN I AM FREED
FROM THIS EXISTENCE
KNOWN
TO ME AS DEATH
WHEN MY SOUL IS SET FREE
FROM THIS DARK PRISON
CALLED LIFE
WHEN MY SOUL IS SET FREE
TO TRAVEL
TO
THE STARS
VENUS AND MARS
WHEN MY SOUL TRAVELS ROADS
WHERE
THE WIND DARE NOT GO
WHEN DEATH GIVES ME LIFE
ONLY THEN WILL I BE
FREE

7TH BIRTHDAY

CONGRATULATIONS
ON YOUR BIRTHDAY
YOU GOT TO BE KIDDING
7 YEARS
EH
7 YEARS
EH
MY TIME DOES FLY
WHY
IT CANNOT BE MORE THAN
A FEW WEEKS AGO
WHEN
I BENT OVER YOUR MOTHER
WE GOT US A BOY
YEP
A BOY
HIS NAME IS
SCOTT ANTHONY CARREON

ENEMY

YOU MAKE ME ANGRY
I WON'T CRAWL
WHILE TODAY YOU RUN THE SHOW
A NEW TOMORROW IS MY GOAL
YOUR GRINNING FACE
BRINGS FORTH ALL MY HATES
SOMETIMES
I FEAR I WILL LOSE MY FAITH
SMILING I SAY GOOD DAY
WALK AWAY PRAYING
YOU BE AROUND
WHEN
I AM THE LEADER
YOU
THE CLOWN

© copyright 2010 Jesse Carreon

COLORS

COLORS
FLOWING BEFORE MY EYES
THEIR SMELL
I CANNOT REALIZE
THEY ARE TRYING
HARD TO RUN ME DOWN
I FOOLED THEM
I GOT MY CLOWN
HE
MY SUPER SUPER MAN
WILL SEE NO ONE
LAYS A HAND ON ME
COLORS
PLEASE GO AWAY
I NEED MORE ROOM TO PLAY
TRAVELING THROUGH
ENDLESS TIME
UP AHEAD I SEE MY MIND
SLOW DOWN WAIT FOR ME
YOU ARE SUPER CHARGED
I SEE

WAR DEAD

SOFT WIND BLOWING
IN THE DIRECTION OF HOME
TELL ALL THOSE PEOPLE
WHERE MY HEART BELONGED
NOT LONG AGO
FROM THESE DISTANT SHORES
FACING THE WIND
MY HEART LONGED TO GO
SOFT WIND BLOWING
IN THE DIRECTION OF HOME
TELL ALL THOSE PEOPLE
I'LL SOON BE HOME
I AM NOW SEEING
MY LAST SUNSET
SOFT WIND BLOWING
IN THE DIRECTION OF HOME
TELL ALL THOSE PEOPLE
I DIDN'T HAVE TO DIE
SOFT WIND BLOWING
IN THE DIRECTION OF HOME
CARRY ME PAST MY HOME
TAKE MY SOUL
BACK TO WHERE IT
BELONGS

© copyright 2010 Jesse Carreon

LADY

LONELY LADY
PASSING THE TIME AWAY
YOUR PRETTY FACE
LONG AGO ERASED
YOUR FACE
ALL ETCHED WITH LINES
BOUGHT
WITH PLEASURES
LATE AT NIGHT
NOT SO LONG AGO

FRIDAY AFTERNOON

FRIDAY AFTERNOON
RAIN FALLING
COMING DOWN
PASSING TIME
WATCHING
TRUCKS AND CARS GO BY
SWEET DREAMS OF YESTERDAY
BRING A SMILE TO MY FACE
I KNOW IT WON'T BE LONG
SOON
YOU WILL BE BY MY SIDE

COLD TUESDAY

NOTHING
HAS COME MY WAY
I LIVE IN LOST DREAMS
OF YESTERDAY
EARLY TUESDAY MORNING
BEFORE THE SUN WAS DUE
IN MY BED I LAID
LOST AGAIN
NOT KNOWING WHAT TO DO
CLOUDS COVERING THE NOON DAY SUN
I KNEW I WOULD BE NEXT IN LINE
COLD TUESDAY
YOU HAVE SHOWN
SHOWN ME THE WAY
WEDNESDAY MORNING
NOT ALL WILL BE THE SAME
A COLD LONELY BODY
NO ONE IS TO BLAME

THE GRAVE

THE
SUN IS BRIGHT
IN EARLY AFTERNOON
A BREEZE
ATTACKING THE LEAVES ON A TREE
HURRYING TRASH ON ITS WAY
AND
CARRYING SOUNDS FROM FAR AWAY
MUTED VOICES
MECHANICAL SOUNDS OF METAL
WHINING SOUND OF RUBBER
SCREECHING ON A ROADWAY
OVERHEAD
THE CONSTANT SOUND OF AIRPLANES
GOING UP
COMING DOWN
WHITE CONTRAILS
FAR UP AND AWAY
EVIDENCE OF AN AIRPORT
NEARBY
MY HEART STRINGS
TWANGING A SAD REFRAIN
A SADNESS I KNOW
WILL NOT GO AWAY
MEMORIES LIKE THE WIND
IN CONSTANT FLOW

A PAINTING OF YEARS PASSED
78 YEARS
4 CHILDREN
AND A WIFE
A SPECK IN THE SEA OF TIME
HE NOW
LIES IN A BED OF DIRT
DAD
I HAVE TO GO
YOU I KNOW
I KNOW WILL REMAIN

CREATION

THE STILLNESS
OF THE TREES
WAS BROKEN
BY THE SHOCK CREATED
THE GEOMETRIC FLIGHT PATTERN
OF THE GEESE FLYING SOUTH
WAS BROKEN
BY THE SHOCK CREATED
HIGH ABOVE
THE TOP OF THE UNIVERSE
HOT AND DENSE PLASMA
SHOOK AND RIPPLED
THE WHOLE WORLD
NOTICE
IN UNISON AS IF ONE
THEY LOOKED
ALL THE POWERS
ALL THE ENERGIES
ALL THE MIGHTY
ALL WHO IS
OR
HAS AND WILL BE
SHOOK
IN A PLACE
NOT KNOWN

TWO BODIES
A MAN
A WOMAN
EMBRACED IN HOT PASSION
LOVE
THE CREATOR
OF ALL CREATORS
WISDOM OF ALL WISDOM
PERMITTED
ALL
NOW AND FOREVER
TO WITNESS
THE EGG FROM THE WOMAN
JOIN
THE SPERM FROM MAN
LIFE
WAS CREATED

DREAM #3

I AM SEARCHING
FOR A DREAM
IMPOSSIBLE TO FIND
I KNOW IT EXISTS
I SEE IT IN MY MIND
I AM SEARCHING FOR HOPE
SOMEHOW MISPLACED
ALL THIS FEAR AND MISTRUST
MUST GIVE WAY TO A BETTER DAY
I AM SEARCHING FOR LOVE
LONG OVERLOOKED
LAYING IN WAIT FOR
ME OR YOU
I AM SEARCHING
IN MY FANCY DREAM
I CAN SEE ME STRUGGLE
I CAN SEE ME SCREAM
I AM SEARCHING

DON'T CRY

DON'T CRY
I'M DYING
DRY YOUR TEARS
KEEP SMILING
WE ALL HAVE TO DIE
NO USE WONDERING
OR ASKING
WHY
I SAY GOODBYE
TO ONE AND ALL
TIME IS DRAWING NEAR
WILL YOU SMILE
WILL YOU KISS ME
ONCE AGAIN
MY DEAR
SLOWLY CLOSE THE DOOR
KEEP WALKING
DON'T LOOK BACK
YOU ARE ALIVE
SMILE
I'M SORRY
I COULD NOT WAIT

COLD WINDY DAY

LONELY SOUNDS
AMPLIFIED
BY THE BARENESS OF THE TREES
FAR AWAY
ECHOES OF CASCADING WATER
A BIRD LOOKING
FOR A PLACE TO HIDE
MUFFLED MAN STEPS
MUMBLED VOICES
BAMBI FROZEN
A STATUE
RUN BAMBI RUN
FAITH
WILL NOT BE KIND TO YOU
TODAY

WORRY

IS THERE A WAY OUT
TO
A PLACE WHERE
ALL DOUBT
ALL FEARS
MELT
LIKE FOG
WITH THE NOONDAY
SUN

NOT LAZY

SOME LOOK AT ME
LAUGH AND CRITICIZE
A DREAMER
SO THEY SAY
ALL THEIR LIVES
THEY WORKED AND FOUGHT
FOR REASONS
THEY MISUNDERSTOOD
HAPPINESS AND PEACE
IS HARD TO FIND
LOVE MONEY POWER
IS NOT THE CURE
THEY THOUGHT IT BE
SMELL THE FLOWERS
PLAY WITH THE CLOUDS
WATCH THE BIRDS
PEACE

LOST SOUL

MY MIND
IS A MILLION MILES AWAY
WITHIN A VOID
MY SOUL
WHO CAN TELL
OUT IN THE PASTURE
AMONG THE FLOWER AND TREES
LOOKING FOR A HOME
SEARCHING
FOREVER MAYBE
IF NOT
FOR
A LITTLE WHILE

MEXICAN

AIN'T NO WAY
YOU CAN WASH MY MIND
MY BROWN SKIN
AIN'T A GOOD SUNTAN
YOUR GRADE SCHOOLS
YOUR HIGH SCHOOLS
YOUR UNIVERSITIES
YOUR TV OR RADIO
YOUR WHITE GOD
YOUR WHITE CHURCH
YOUR WHITE UNIVERSE
LOOK AT ME
FRONT
SIDE
BACK
TOP OR BOTTOM
INTELLECTUALLY OR SPIRITUALLY
YOU AIN'T GONNA DO IT
I AM A MEXICAN

HUMILITY

I AM GOING TO SHAKE HANDS
WITH JESUS
I AM GOING TO SAY HI
TO MY LORD
I AM GOING TO THANK
MY LORD
AND
IF HE IS NICE
I'LL ASK FOR MORE
YES YES
I'M MEETING SWEET JESUS
YES YES
I WILL SEE HIM ONCE MORE
I AM GOING TO SHAKE HANDS
WITH JESUS
I AM GOING TO SAY HI
TO MY LORD

© copyright 2010 Jesse Carreon

PEACE # 2

LOOK AROUND
NOTHING
PEACE
IS A
MILLION MILES
AWAY
MOSQUITOES
HUMIDITY
SMELLS
JUNGLE SOUNDS
DEATH LURKING
MAN HUNTING MAN
AN EERIE QUIET
IN THE MIDST OF WAR

SLEEPING BABY

DREAM MY LITTLE
ONE
DREAM SWEET DREAMS
MUCH TOO SOON
YOU WILL BE AWAKEN
TO A WORLD
I RATHER LEAVE UNSAID
DREAM MY LITTLE ONE
MY LOVE FOR YOU
WILL NOT ERASE
THE HUMAN RACE
STANDING HERE
BESIDE YOUR BED
I SLOWLY
TOUCH YOUR
LITTLE HEAD

MOON

MOON
ONCE UNTOUCHED
BY HUMAN HANDS
A VIRGIN
A PAINTING
BRIGHT LIGHT
OF THE NIGHT TIME
SKY
LUCKY YOU
MAN HAS ARRIVED
TO SET YOU FREE
EONS
EONS YOU HAVE
LAID IN PEACE
A WARNING
IF I MAY BE BOLD TO SPEAK
COUNSEL
FROM ONE WHO'S SEEN
MAN'S
TAINTED BRUSH
AND
TAINTED PAINT

IDIOT

AN IDIOT
ONCE STOOD
ATOP
OF THE WORLD
LOOKED AROUND
SMILED
SAID
WHAT A SHOW

HITCHHIKING

COLD WIND BLOWING
WARMTH AWAY FROM ME
A CONCRETE TONGUE
MILES AND MILES I SEE
THE QUIET AND LONELINESS
OF A DARK DARK NIGHT
MILES I CAN SEE
NO CARS IN SIGHT
SPECK OF LIGHT
FAR AWAY I SEE
MAYBE
A
FATHER MOTHER CHILD
A FAMILY
COLD WIND BLOWING
IN THIS DARK DARK NIGHT
AMIDST THIS
LONELINESS
A SHOOTING STAR
LIGHT UP THE NIGHT

HITCHHIKING #2

I STAND ALONE
WAITING
WAITING FOR A BUS
COLD WIND
BLOWING
MY HAND AND FEET ARE COLD
COLD WIND
DRAWING TEARS DOWN MY FACE
SNOW STARTED FALLING
THE HOLES IN MY SHOES
ARE TRYING TO MAKE ME
SING THE BLUES
TWO O'CLOCK IN THE MORNING
IT MUST BE CHRISTMAS DAY
AND
I'VE STILL A LONG LONG
WAY TO GO

BODIES

LOOK AT THE BODIES
SEE HOW THEY MOVE
THEIR EMPTY MINDS
IN ANOTHER ROOM
ROBOTS
PAINTED SHELLS
NO RHYME OR REASON
MECHANICAL
HITHER AND THITHER
IN A RUSH TO GO
NOWHERE

FLOWERS

FLOWERS
OF MANY COLORS
MAKE THE WORLD BRIGHTER
SILENTLY STANDING
A BEAUTY
A COLLECTION OF
YELLOWS BLUES REDS
COLORS WITH NO NAME
FREE NO CHARGE
FOR ALL TO SEE
HOME TO MANY
JOY TO SOME
DREADING WINTER
WHEN THEY WILL BE GONE
COLOR ERASED

© copyright 2010 Jesse Carreon

FUNERAL FOR MY FRIEND'S BROTHER

WORDS
WORTHLESS EUPHEMISM
OF OUR INNER EMOTIONS
YOUNG BUDDING TREE
MORE DAYS
WERE NOT MEANT FOR YOU
USELESS RITUALS
TRY TO COMPROMISE
PASSIONS
THAT CANNOT BE SEEN
WITH HUMAN EYES
LIFE IS FULL
OF SORROW

© copyright 2010 Jesse Carreon

BUS STATION

PRETTY GIRL
WAITING
AT THE BUS STATION
I WONDER
YOUR DESTINATION
COULD
COULD I SPEAK TO YOU
I AM
MILES AND MILES
FROM HOME
ALL ALONE
ALONE LIKE YOU
A KIND WORD
A TENDER SMILE
IF ONLY
YOU TURN AROUND
COFFEE'S COLD
NO PLACE TO GO
TURN AROUND
TURN AROUND
OH OH OH

ALONE

WITH NO ONE
I MUST FACE DEATH
A LONESOME MOMENT
PARDON ME
I MUST CONFESS
I WISH IT WERE NOT TO BE
NOT LONG AGO
I ARRIVED SCREAMING
THE WORLD KNEW
IT SAW MY EYES
NO MORE MORNINGS
NO MORE NOTHING
A WORLD
ASKING ME TO DIE
ALONE WITH NONE
I MUST FACE DEATH
ALONE
I'LL SEE THE SUN
SLOWLY COME TO REST

REGRETS

MEMORIES FLOW
FASTER THAN WATER
RUSHING OVER A WATERFALL
THE YEARS
CRASHING IN A HEAP
YOUTH
HAS COME AND GONE
NOW AS THE SUN SETS
I SEE
WITH A MORE CLEAR
LIGHT
I NOW UNDERSTAND
MY YEARS
COULD HAVE BEEN USED
MORE WISELY
AND
WITH MORE HONESTY

CONVERSATION

DEATH:
    I'VE DECIDED YOU CAN WAIT
DEFEAT:
    I'VE DECIDED YOU CAN WAIT
SELF:
    DON'T CRAWL YOU ARE A MAN

EARLY MORNING

EARLY MORNING
SUN SHINING
THROUGH THE WINDOW
LAZY SLEEPY HEAD
RATHER STAY IN BED
EXTRA MOMENTS
WITH MY LOVE
SHE
CAME INTO MY LIFE
AN ACCIDENT
A LIGHT
MY SILVER LINING
PRECIOUS
FOOD OF LOVE
HOURS SPENT
EXPLORING
THE MANY WONDERS
OF
A MAN AND WOMAN
IN LOVE

RANDOM THOUGHT

THE TREES ARE GREEN
THE SKY IS BLUE
THE SUN SHINES
HAIR TOSSED
BY THE HOWLING WIND
THE TRAFFIC LIGHT
IS STILL GREEN
CARS
NEW CLOTHES
PEOPLE LAUGHING
WITHIN THE MOTHER'S WOMB
LIFE IS WROUGHT

COUNTRY SONG

HERE I AM LISTENING TO
A HANK WILLIAMS SONG
"COLD COLD HEART"
MY PROBLEMS MELTED
TWO BLOODY MARYS
REPRIEVE
TWO HOURS OF REST
MY MIND AT PEACE

DEAD SOLDIERS

LOOK SEE ME CRY
WHILE MY BROTHERS
ON A BATTLEFIELD
DIE
HOW MANY TEARS
HOW MANY KILLED
POOR MAN
CAN'T YOU SEE
THIS WORLD
IS A TEMPORARY
STAND
THE PROUD WORD
MUST BE DEFENDED
THOUGH
GOOD SENSE DON'T
DEMAND IT
SHADES OF COLORS
COMING BEFORE MY EYES
MY SIMPLE MIND
CANNOT
UNDERSTAND WHY

DAD

AGE
HAS FORCED ME TO REEVALUATE
MY DAD
THAT DULL SEMI-DUNCE MAN
HAS TURNED INTO A GENIUS
SPANKINGS ARE NOW RECALLED
I MUST ADMIT I DESERVED ONE AND ALL
AN EMPTY CHAIR AT SUPPER TIME
HOT DAYS COLD DAYS
HE WORKED 14 HOURS A DAY
ARGUMENTS AND FIGHTS
MY SMART MOUTH COCKY SELF
I KNEW ALL THE ANSWERS
HOWEVER
NOT THE QUESTIONS
HARD SO HARD I TRIED
TO YANK THAT YOKE
SET ME FREE
NOW
IN AFTERTHOUGHT
I AM GLAD
HE HAD A STRONGER HAND
A CROOKED ROAD HE MADE STRAIGHT
WE
ARE DIFFERENT AS DAY TO NIGHT
THAT MAN AND I
HE SEES BLACK I SEE WHITE
AGE
HAS OPENED MY EYES
NOW
WELL I SEE
I AM
I
BECAUSE OF HE

UNTITLED

LOST THOUGHT
ON A RAINY DAY
A HELPING HAND
FOR MY FALLEN FRIEND
HELP HIM UP
HE IS A MAN
TORN AND TATTERED
CLOTHES
SUNKEN EYES
LOST SMILE
CROOKED TEETH
DIRTY
BAD SMELL
HIS TROUBLES AND PAIN
WE DO NOT SHARE
HELP HIM STAND
NO MATTER HIS NAME
A HELPING HAND
FOR MY FALLEN FRIEND
TIME WILL NOT GIVE US
A SECOND LOOK
YOUR FANCY WORDS
MUST
BE PUT TO WORK

HOPE

THERE
IS A BRIGHTER DAY
FOR YOU MY FRIEND
MANY TIMES
WE DO NOT UNDERSTAND
ALL THE PAIN AND HATE
IN OUR LAND
BITTER TEARS SHED TODAY
WILL BRING A BRIGHTER DAY
SOMEONE MUST ALWAYS
PAY A PRICE
THERE
ARE MAN WHO ALONE
HAVE TO DIE
A MOTHER
MUST PAY THE PRICE
FOR A CHILD TO HAVE LIFE
WE LIVE IN A TIME
WHEN SOME LAUGH
OTHERS CRY

LIFE

LIFE
WHY CAN I NOT
MAKE YOU SEE
YOU
WILL BE THE END OF ME
IF YOU BY CHANCE
HAD NOT COME MY WAY
I
WOULD NOT BE HERE TODAY
IF
BY CHANCE I HAD A CHOICE
A VOID A DREAM A TREE
IS WHAT I RATHER BE
LIFE
I HOPE YOU SEE
SOMEDAY
YOU
WILL BE THE END OF ME

A TREE BY THE CREEK

THERE WAS A TIME
AS
A YOUNG MAN
I WOULD SIT
BENEATH
A TREE BY THE CREEK
CLEAR MY MIND PLAN MY LIFE
I LIVED
MY LIFE A THOUSAND TIMES
BENEATH THAT TREE
A HOLLOW FOR MY MIND
OF
SAFETY AND STRENGTH
MY FIRST TASTE OF LOVE
WAS BENEATH THAT TREE
A FEELING SUCH
I CANNOT EXPLAIN
RECKLESS AND CARELESS
I WAS
IN THIS GAME OF LOVE
BROKEN PROMISES
FALSE HOPES
DEAD DREAMS
ENDLESS DAYS
BENEATH THAT TREE
I WOULD SIT
LICKING MY WOUNDS
SEARCHING FOR SEARCH

IT MUST HAVE BEEN
SHORT OF ETERNITY
WHEN SHE CAME TO ME
SHE GAVE ME HOPE
SHE GAVE ME LOVE
SHE GAVE ME PEACE
IT WAS A SUNDAY
WHEN
I CUT DOWN THE TREE
IT FELL ACROSS THE CREEK

HELP # 10

HELP: I AM ON MY WAY DOWN
HELP: I KNOW ALL IS NOT WELL
HELP: I SEE HIM
HELP: HE WANTS ME TO BE HIS CLOWN
HELP: HE IS DRAGGING ME DOWN
HELP: LIFE DO NOT LET ME DOWN
HELP: A HAND IS ALL I NEED
HELP: GOD GOD HELP
OH WELL
I AM ON MY WAY TO
HELL

john

YOU DON'T HAVE TO SAY
SORRY
DON'T WORRY SAYING
GOODBYE
YOU GO YOUR WAY
I MINE
WE MAY MEET
SOME OTHER DAY
REMEMBER MY NAME IS
John

UGH UGH

SOME PLACE
DOWN THE ROAD OF CREATION
WHERE FAITH FIRST HAD
ITS ORDINATION
HOPE CRAWLING
LOOKING TO BE FOUND
A HELPING HAND
FOR THE NEW BORN
A NEW BIRTH
A NEW LOVE
FOR A TROUBLED NATION
AROUND THE CORNER
BY THE EDGE OF TIME
A DEAD SOUL
ASKING
FOR ANOTHER TRY
SOME PLACE
DOWN THE ROAD OF CREATION
A NEW BORN
NEW HOPE
FOR
A TROUBLE NATION
AIN'T
NO USE IN THE DEAD
CRYING

HEY LORD

HEY LORD
LOOK AT ME
HEY LORD
WHAT DO YOU SEE
NOTHING
NOTHING IS ME
I AM A DREAM
WITH NO END
IF YOU GET HOLD OF ME
TURN ME
INTO A TREE

LOVE

LOVE IS NOT EASY
LOVE IS COMPLICATED
SOUL TEARING
I AM NOT A god
I HURT
I ACHE
LOVE
IS NOT EASY

DREAM #99

I FIRST SAW HIM
OUTSIDE MY CAR WINDOW
STANDING
IN THE MIDDLE OF NOWHERE
IN THE RAIN
ALONE AND FORGOTTEN
EYES HEAVY
WITH PAIN AND SORROW
IN A VOICE
MORE FELT
THAN HEARD
HE CRIED
PEACE AND LOVE
TO ALL
NO FRIENDS OR ENEMIES
NONE
I COULD SEE
ONLY HE AND ME
HEAVY EYES
PAINTED ON MY REAR VIEW MIRROR
AWAKING MEMORIES
OF WORDS
ROUGHLY SPOKEN
A LONG TIME AGO
CRUCIFY HIM
CRUCIFY HIM

WORLD

IF
THE WORLD WOULD
LISTEN
I
WOULD SHOUT
THERE HAS
GOT TO BE MORE
THAN
THIS LIFE

DEAD DOG

I THOUGHT
I SAW A DEAD DOG EAT A BABY
WHO KNOWS
IT COULD HAVE BEEN
MY IMAGINATION
MAYBE
HA HA HA
I SAW A BABY
EAT A DEAD DOG
MY FRIEND THIS IS NO JOKE
HA HA HA
LOOK AROUND
CAN YOU SEE
THE ONE TELLING THE TRUTH
IS ME
HA HA HA

CHURCH

GO TO CHURCH
BURN IT DOWN
HOLINESS
WILL BE ALL AROUND
AND
IF WHAT SCIENCE
SAYS IS TRUE
A LITTLE HOLINESS
WILL COME TO YOU

A MEMORY

IF I MAY
I WOULD LIKE TO SAY
YOUR EYES
REMIND ME OF A GIRL
FROM ANOTHER DAY
SHE CAME TO ME
JUST IN TIME
OTHERWISE
I WOULD HAVE LOST
MY MIND
SHE GAVE ME HOPE
SHE MADE ME SMILE
SHE WAS MINE
FOR A LITTLE WHILE
THAT WAS
A LONG TIME AGO
AND
LIKE THE WINTER SNOW
SHE WAS GONE
WITH
THE FIRST DAY OF SPRING

COLORS # 2

WILL YOU
SPEND SOME TIME WITH ME
I'LL PAINT
BOTH
THE SUN AND THE SEA
WITH COLORS
YOU HAVE NEVER SEEN
AND
IF IN TIME
THOSE COLORS FADE
I WON'T CRY
WHEN YOU WALK AWAY

© copyright 2010 Jesse Carreon

FAREWELL

FAREWELL TO LIFE
YOU
ARE TO MY SOUL
WHAT
FOOD IS TO MY BODY
ONLY A NECESSITY
NOT
AN END

© copyright 2010 Jesse Carreon

DREAM # 101

FORGOTTEN DREAM
FROM MY LOST YOUTH
NOON DAY SUN
HIDDEN BY THE DARK CLOUDS
THE SPARROW UNDECIDED
WHERE TO RIDE OUT THE STORM
MYSELF IN BED
COUNTING THE SECONDS AS LIGHTNING
STREAKS
ACROSS THE SKY
FOR A MOMENT
I COULD SEE HER FACE
I COULD HEAR HER VOICE
MEMORIES
OF A LOST DAY A LOST HOUR
IS IT A YEAR
YOU
ONCE AGAIN TOUCHED MY HEART
A STREAK OF SUNLIGHT
FIGHTING PAST THE WASTED CLOUDS
LIGHTNING STREAKS NOW FARAWAY
THE LOUD THUNDER
NOW A SOFT RUMBLE
FROM
BENEATH THE MAIL BOX
THE SPARROW ESCAPES
ONCE AGAIN
READY
TO CHALLENGE THE
SKY

BRIGHT MOON

HALF PAST MIDNIGHT
ON A MOONLIT NIGHT
THE SUN FORGOT
TO SET
IT JUST
CHANGED ITS MASK
AND NAME

QUESTION

HOW
CAN I SEE TOMORROW
IF I DO NOT
BELIEVE IN TODAY
HOW
CAN I LOVE
IF
ALL I KNOW IS
HATE

BLACK BIRD

BLACK BIRD
HIGH
HIGH
SILHOUETTE AGAINST
THE MORNING SKY
BLACK BIRD
HIGH
TOGETHER
YOU AND THE SUN
TOGETHER
YOU
DRIFT THROUGH SPACE
I
MY BODY MY FEET
FIRMLY ON THE GROUND
I
ENVY YOU

CONFESSION

I HAVE OFTEN
ENJOYED LOOKING
AT
THE BEAUTY
OF ROSES

I SEE

I SEE
WITH THE EYES OF A god
I HEAR
WITH THE EARS OF A god
I LOVE
WITH THE LOVE OF A god

MY WIFE

SHE SAT
NAKED
AS THE DAY SHE WAS BORN
WET MATTED HAIR
WATER RUNNING DOWN
HER BACK AND CHEEKS
MIRROR IN HAND
ADMIRING GOD'S HANDY WORK
FIRST
SHE COMBS HER HAIR
SECOND
SHE CHECKS HER TEETH
PRIMPING
ENJOYING HERSELF
WELL SATISFIED
WITH WHAT SHE SAW
I WAS TOO

POPCORN

I
HAVE OFTEN
AT NIGHT
GAZED STARED
AT INFINITY
BEYOND THE STARS
YES
INTO THE PLAY GROUND
OF THE gods
I
HAVE COME
TO THIS CONCLUSION
IT IS
ALIKE
TO POPCORN
90 % AIR
10 % SUBSTANCE

OLD GIRLFRIEND

DON'T LOOK BACK
JUST
WALK OUT THE DOOR
I GOT ME A NEW LOVE
I DON'T WANT THE NEIGHBORS
TO KNOW
YOU THOUGHT YOURSELF A DOLLAR
YOU ARE
ONLY
LOOSE CHANGE

MAKING LOVE TO JANIS

WE
TOUCH OUR BODIES
IN MANNER AND PLACES
OTHERS
MAY NOT
WE
WHISPER WORDS
AND
DARK SECRETS
IN THE NIGHT
WE
SMILE
LAUGH
LOVE
TILL BOTH
BECOME ONE

50

THE SUN GOES UP
THE SUN COMES DOWN
THE WORLD KEEPS TURNING 'ROUND
YOU ARE ON MY MIND
THE NIGHT COMES THEN IT IS GONE
THE FLOWERS CONTINUE TO BLOOM
    YOU ARE ON MY MIND
IN THE EARLY HOURS
BEFORE THE BREAK OF DAWN
I BRING YOU FLOWERS
FRESH AS A NEW DAY DAWN
I HAVE TRIED
NOT SUCCEEDED
AND
AS I LEAVE
THIS COLD CEMETERY
I WISH TOO
I WERE DEAD

UNTITLED

THE MIRROR REFLECTED
AN EMPTY FACE
THE EYES THE WINDOW
TO THE SOUL
VACANT AND NON FOCUSED
CONCEALING
AN INNER BATTLE
WITHIN MY SOUL
A CONTINUOUS FIGHT
IN THE SEARCH OF
WHAT
TRUTH AND BEING
THIS GNAWING OF
MY SOUL
A CONTINUOUS BATTLE
OF CHOICES TO BE
MADE
OPEN
MY EYES JESUS
THE GOD
HEAR MY ANGUISHED CRY
THIS BATTLE
I AM LOSING

FOR MY WIFE JANIS

(I was in Minnesota away from home)
WE ARE TWO SPECKS
OF DUST
IN A MILLION STARS
WE ARE TWO PEOPLE
OF
A
BILLION BILLION
WHO HAVE WALKED
THIS EARTH
AND
FOR A REASON
WE WERE UNITED
BY OUR
CREATOR

© copyright 2010 Jesse Carreon

A THOUGHT

I CAN
HEAR COTTON CALLING
I CAN
HEAR SUMMER CALL MY NAME
THE SUN SHINES
BIRDS CALL ME BROTHER
WILD DOGS
KNOW MY NAME
SEE THE
WATER SOOTHINGLY FLOWING
SEE THE
GRASS A BRIGHT GREEN
WHEN THE WIND
TURNS
BLOWS FROM THE NORTH
YOU KNOW WINTER
IS NEAR

SATURDAY NIGHT

WELL
IT IS SATURDAY NIGHT
WE
ARE SHOPPING AT A STORE
BUYING THIS OR THAT
ME, MY WIFE AND KIDS
THE TWINS ARE RUNNING
HELTER SKELTER
GETTING
INTO ALL IMAGINABLE TROUBLE
MY OLDEST BOY
CHALLENGES ALL OTHER BOYS
INTO
ONE THING OR ANOTHER
OR
ARE THEY SOLVING
A WORLD PROBLEM
CAN'T SAY
I DO KNOW
WE ARE AT PEACE
A MAN
CANNOT ASK FOR MORE
THE SOUND OF THE CASH REGISTER
THE SMELL OF POPCORN
FILLS THE AIR
IF
I CLOSE MY EYES
I
SWEAR IT IS A CIRCUS

WAR

MY SOUL
REEKS OF A SMELL
KNOWN WELL
TO ME
BREWED IN DIPLOMATIC
CHANNELS
FESTERED IN BOARDROOMS
A FLAW
IN OUR EFFORTS TO
COMMUNICATE
MY SOUL REEKS
OF
OIL AND STEEL

A WHITE VINYL

IT COVERS
HOUSES
TREES
CARS
AND ALL
THE MISPLACED
WHITE COTTON CLOUD
OF SUMMER
REFLECTED FROM THE GROUND
THE WATER PELLETS
A
WELCOME VISITOR
INCLUDING THE INCONVENIENCE
IT TRANSFORMS
THE UGLY TO BEAUTY
THE BEAUTIFUL
INTO A WONDER

DREAMING

DREAMING A DREAM
TOO LONG
PRAYING AND HOPING
THE LOOK IN YOUR EYES
SAYS
I'VE BEEN SO WRONG
TOMORROW
YOU WILL BE GONE
I
CANNOT HEAR THE WORD
YOU WILL NOT SAY
SORRY
I LOVED YOU
NIGHT AND DAY
THE SUN
DON'T SHINE
NOT ALL THE TIME
YOUR LOVE I KNOW
WILL NOT BE MINE

ANOTHER THOUGHT

I WONDER IF TODAY
I COULD FIND A WAY
TO
UNDERSTAND MANKIND
IF
BY CHANCE I COULD
CHANGE THIS WORLD
A LITTLE
IF
BY WORDS I COULD
END WAR
END HUNGER
END HATE
JUST
A THOUGHT NOT MORE

ME

MANY A TIME I'VE STUMBLED
MANY A TIME I'VE BEEN WRONG
MORE THAN ONCE I CRIED
LATE INTO THE NIGHT
IN THE MORNING
I WILL FACE AND FIGHT
ANOTHER DAY
ONLY I CAN SEE
THROUGH MY EYES
I WILL MY BEST
LET TIME
AND
THE ALMIGHTY
BE MY JUDGE
NOT YOU

IMMIGRANT

ONE BY ONE
THEY KNEW NO ONE
ON
WHOSE HELP THEY COULD DEPEND
SOME WITHERED
WHILE OTHERS GREW STRONG
A JOURNEY
THEY DID TAKE
TO THE LAND OF WONDERS AND HOPE
SEARCHING
FOR A HELPING HAND
ON
THEIR FACE THE DOOR WAS SLAMMED
DO NOT WALK AWAY
DO NOT LOOK
THE ROAD IS LONG
IF THE BATTLE
IS TO BE WON

EVOLUTION A THOUGHT

WHEN
AND IF I COULD
WILLED
AND
ALL WOULD BE MISUNDERSTOOD
TAKE SIMPLICITY
BAKE
A COMPLICATED CAKE
PLACING
IT UPON THE GROUND
SIT AND WAIT
FOR MAN TO BE
BORN

TOMORROW

IS ANOTHER DAY
I SIT IN MY ROOM
ALONE
THINKING
COLD RAIN
KEEPS
COMING DOWN
TEMPERATURE
GETTING COLDER
TV
IS ON THE MEND
I NEED
THIS MONTH'S RENT
TOMORROW
IS ANOTHER DAY
MAYBE
THE SUN WILL SHINE

A LOST TIME

I
STILL REMEMBER
SWEET
LATE SEPTEMBERS
WITH
YOU BY MY SIDE
LOVE WAS OUR GUIDE
SWEET DREAMS OF YOUTH
COME AND GONE
LIFE
WITH ITS MEMORIES
MUST GO ON
I WILL ALWAYS REMEMBER
THOSE
SWEET SEPTEMBERS
WHEN LOVE WAS LIVING
AND
KISSES FREELY GIVEN

BOUGHT LOVE

YOUR
LOVE IS NOT TRUE
YOUR
HEART WANDERS
YOU
LIKE MY DOG
GO
FROM TREE TO TREE
NOT
SURE WHERE TO BE
YOU
AWAKE IN THE MORNING
ASKING MY NAME
YOU
SWEAR I'M NOT JACK
MAYBE SAM
YOU
SAY YOU LOVE ME
YOU
CALL MY NAME
A FOOL I AM
I'LL
TRY TO UNDERSTAND

DREAM #104

I CANNOT SEE
MY EYES ARE GONE
I GREET DARKNESS
WITH A SMILE
A NEW FRIEND
A NEW WORLD
A NEW THOUGHT
I'LL NOT CRY
NOR WILL I ASK TO DIE
INSTEAD
I ONCE MORE
WILL
BECOME A CHILD

© copyright 2010 Jesse Carreon

DARK MOOD

WHEN
THE SUN SHINES TOMORROW
I
DO NOT KNOW WHERE
I WILL BE
THE FUTURE
HOLDS NO PROMISE
THE PAST
WELL IT HAD TO BE
MANY THINK ME
A CLOWN
I SEE NO REASON
FOR ME
TO STICK AROUND
MAYBE TOMORROW
LIFE WITH A PURPOSE
MAYBE NOT
TOMORROW
I DO NOT KNOW
WHERE I WILL BE
DEAD
MAYBE

FOREVER

FOREVER ON A PROMISE
THROUGH
SICKNESS AND SORROW
TOGETHER
WE FACE
TOMORROW
HAND IN HAND
WE MAY NOT UNDERSTAND
WHY
SOME LIVE OTHERS DIE
YOU AND I
SOMETIMES WILL CRY
LIFE PROBLEMS
A MAJOR BURDEN
MANY BATTLES
WILL BE FOUGHT
SOME LOST
I'M NOT WORRIED
IF
YOU ARE BY MY SIDE

DREAM # 103

I HEAR FOOTSTEPS
NEARBY
CAN IT BE DEATH
I CAN FEEL
A PRESENCE
    A BODY
NEXT TO ME
CAN IT BE MY BODY
IS THIS A DREAM
IS THIS REAL
WOW
AM I DEAD

DREAM # 104

ANOTHER DREAM
IT HAS BEEN PREORDAINED
MAN MUST WORK
FOR A BETTER LIFE
WOULD
IT NOT BE A JOKE
IF LIFE WAS A DREAM

I AM A CHRISTIAN

CHRIST IS MY SAVIOR
I LOVE CHRIST
IN A BOOK A TALLY
OF MY SINS IS KEPT
FULL AND WELL WORN
A BURDEN
I
NO LONGER
ABLE TO CARRY
LOST
DISILLUSIONED
IN ANGER I CRIED
THESE ARE YOURS
A VOICE IN RETURN
YES
I DIED
A LONG TIME AGO
FOR YOU
I ASK ONLY
YOUR
LOVE
IN RETURN

DREAM # 102

I DREAM OF DEATH
TWICE A MONTH
I FACE DEATH
TWICE A MONTH
I CRY
TWICE A MONTH
I SCREAM
TWICE A MONTH
I FACE REALITY
TWICE A MONTH

THE LIGHT

FARAWAY
THERE IS A LIGHT
THAT SHINES
THROUGH
DIRT AND FILTH
THROUGH
SHAME AND SORROW
IT LIGHTS THE WAY
FOR A NEW TOMORROW

EXASPERATION

CRISS CROSSING CURRENTS
OF FIRE
REACHING THE DEPTHS
OF MY SOUL
    SCREECHING GOUGING SCREAMING
FIERY FINGERS
TEARING AT THE FIBERS OF MY
SELF
SCAB UPON SCAB
SCAR UPON SCAR
BLOOD UPON BLOOD
THE VIOLENT TORRENTS
OF CREATION
THEY HIDE THEY HIDE
SO WELL
I FEEL THEM
IN MY FINGERS
DOWN
TO THE TIP OF MY TOES
SOON IN THE NOT TOO
DISTANT FUTURE
IN MY OLD AGE
I WILL CRY OUT
IN ANGER
'GOD NEXT TIME
DO YOUR JOB WELL'

YOU

YOU
ARE A WARM FIRE
ON A WINTER DAY
YOU
ARE MUSTARD
ON A HOT DOG
YOU
ARE BUTTER
ON MY POPCORN
YOU
ARE A COOL DRINK
ON A HOT HOT DAY
YOU
ARE EVERY THING
WHICH MAKES
LIFE A LITTLE SWEETER
MAY I STEAL
A KISS
A KISS
FROM YOUR LIPS
MAY I STEAL
YOUR LOVE
ALL YOUR
LOVE

FIREFIGHT

THE EYE PUPIL
SHARPENED TO A NEEDLE POINT
AN ABERRATION
AN IMAGINATION
NOT A DREAM
A BLACK SHADOW
SILHOUETTE WELL
AGAINST A BLACK NIGHT
A FAINT WHISPER
IN A NOISY ROOM
THE LOUD SHOUT OF SILENCE
MAGNIFIES THE BLACKNESS
OF THE NIGHT
A SWEAT BEAD ROLLING
DOWN A FACE
IN A RACE TO AN END
WITH THE TENSION
RUSHING TO A TRIGGER FINGER
THE QUIETNESS OF THE NIGHT
ITS LOUD SILENCE
AMPLIFIES THE SUDDEN MOVEMENT
OF THE SHADOW
AS IT MULTIPLIES
ITSELF BY 1+4 TILL MANY
THE ADRENALINE RUSHING
IN PREPARATION
FOR SOON THE SILENCE
OF THE NIGHT

WILL BURST IN A CORNUCOPIA
OF
SHARP CRACKS LOUD BOOMS
BURST OF LIGHT DEADLY THUNDER
CONFUSION AND FEAR
LOST IN ITS MIDST
ARE THE PAIN CRIES
AS HUMAN FLESH IS TORN
LIVE BODIES BECOME DEAD
THE GRIM REAPER PLUCKING SOME
OTHERS NOT

ONE WHO REFUSED TO FALL

HE STOOD
TWO FEET UNDER HIM
HE REFUSED TO FALL
TELL HIM
HE HAS NO REASON
TO STAND
HE SINGS A DIFFERENT
SONG
TELL HIM
HE DON'T BELONG
HE STANDS LIKE A god
HE IS NOT
TELL HIM TO FALL
TELL HIM TO FALL
OH GOD
PLEASE MAKE HIM CRAWL
HE STANDS
TWO FEET ON THE GROUND
HE IS A
MAN

29

LOVE IS ALL AROUND
LOOK AND SEE
LOVE THAT IS MEANT
FOR YOU AND ME
FROM EARLY MORN
TILL LATE EVENING SUN
I'LL SIT AND TELL YOU
YOU ARE THE ONLY ONE
WHO
MAKES THIS LIFE SO DEAR
FOREVER AND A DAY
YOU AND I
TOGETHER
IN THIS LIFE

© copyright 2010 Jesse Carreon

WHO

IF I WERE YOU
AND
YOU WERE I
WOULD
WE LIKE EACH OTHER
IF I COULD SEE MYSELF
AS YOU DO NOW
WOULD I RATHER BE
ANOTHER

© copyright 2010 Jesse Carreon

LOST THOUGHT

IT WAS LOST BY ACCIDENT
NOW
I FIND NO PEACE OF MIND
MY MIND CANNOT UNDERSTAND
WHAT WAS LOST
IS JUST A THOUGHT
SOMEWHERE
FAR OUT IN INFINITY
RACING AND KEEPING TIME
WITH OTHER LOST THOUGHTS
RUNS THAT THOUGHT OF MINE
AND
THIS SHELL CALLED MY
BODY
CANNOT UNDERSTAND
THAT
WHICH WAS LEFT BEHIND

TIME # 4

I HEARD
THROUGH THE WIND
TIME IS NOT ENDLESS
IT ACCUMULATES
INTO NOTHINGNESS
THIS SIDE OF THE HOUSE OF GOD
THE WIND YOU MUST BELIEVE
BECAUSE
WHEN THE WIND BLOWS
THE LEAVES ARE BLOWN
FROM THE TREE
AND
YOU KNOW THAT IS TRUE
OTHERWISE
FALL COULD NOT COME
AFTER SUMMER

NO TITLE

I AM ONE
NOTHING LESS
YOU MAY SAY
NATURE GOT THE BEST
MY EYES STILL CRY
MY HEART IS ALIVE

THE CAT

ONE NIGHT WHILE WAITING
TO FACE THE DAWN
I SAW A CAT COMING
MY WAY
HI SAID I
HELLO SAID HE
AS
HE WALKED BY
MR. CAT SAID I
YOU ARE SO FREE OF CARE
TELL ME
HOW
SO I TOO MAY SHARE

© copyright 2010 Jesse Carreon

I YEAR ANNIVERSARY

WONDERING WHAT TO SAY
A YEAR AGO TODAY
ON OUR WEDDING DAY
YOU ALL DRESSED IN WHITE
WERE TO TAKE ME
YOUR MAN TO BE
    A PROMISE
    FOREVER PLUS A DAY
I THE HOLLOW HERO
ASKING
YOU THE MIGHTY QUEEN
ON ME TO PLACE YOUR FATE
    A PROMISE
    FOREVER PLUS A DAY
NO RICHES TO OFFER
A DREAM TO SHARE
    A PROMISE
    FOREVER PLUS A DAY
ONE DAY TOGETHER
WE EACH CAN SAY
YOU
THANK YOU MY DEAR HUSBAND
I
THANK YOU MY DEAR WIFE
A DREAM TO SHARE
A LIFE TO LIVE
A LOVE TO GIVE
    A PROMISE
    FOREVER PLUS A DAY

A THOUGHT WHILE AT WORK

WHO AM I
I DO CRY
TELL ME QUICK
BEFORE I DIE
IS THAT YOU
OR IS IT I
THE MAN I SEE
IN THAT MILKY SKY
A LIFE I LIVE
I KNOW NOT WHY
ASKING QUESTIONS
BEFORE I DIE
THE TEN
GOLDEN RULES
I HAVE BEEN TOLD
IS ALL I NEED
TO REACH MY GOAL
MANY YEARS HAVE COME AND GONE
SINCE THAT TALE TO MAN BEEN TOLD
OF THE MAN WITH TWO STONES
COME COME
I DO CRY
IS IT NOT A LIE
TELL ME QUICK
BEFORE I DIE

ALONE AT THE BUS STATION

100 PEOPLE GOING
100 DIFFERENT WAYS
SUN IS SHINING
MUST BE IN 100 OTHER PLACES
BARREN TREES SILHOUETTE
AGAINST THE AGGREGATIONS
OF CONCRETE AND STEEL
I SIT ALONE
MANKIND COLD AS STEEL
I MAY AS WELL BE 100 MILE IN SPACE
I AM TO THESE PEOPLE
WHAT A PEBBLE OF SAND
MUST BE
TO ANOTHER PEBBLE OF SAND
100 MILES AWAY

© copyright 2010 Jesse Carreon

THOUGHTS

WHILE MY DAUGHTER
SLEEPS ON MY LAP
I KNOW MANY
WILL CALL ME EMOTIONAL
THE LITERARY WORLD WILL
ACKNOWLEDGE MY WORDS AS JUNK
LET THEM SO BE IT
MY WORDS
I WILL TELL YOU
I LOVE MY SON
I LOVE MY DAUGHTERS
THE TWINS
    I LOVE MY WIFE
I ENJOY BEING WITH THEM
I ENJOY MY SON
I ENJOY LISTENING
TO THE JIBBER JABBER
OF MY 2 YEAR OLD TWINS

FROM AFAR

YOU SEE THEM WALKING
FACELESS BODIES
WANDERING
AS IF LEAVES BLOWN
BY THE WIND
AND IN YOUR PRIDE
YOU PITY THEM
YOU PRAY FOR THEM
YOU WISH THEM WELL
FROM AFAR
FOR YOU FEAR THAT
ABYSS
THE DROP SEEN
PRECIPITOUS AND MYSTERIOUS
A BOTTOM UNSEEN
AN ABYSS
YES YOU FEAR
THAT INNER VOICE
A WARNING
THE DEMARCATION
LINE
IS THIN
THINNER
THAN
YOU MAY THINK

MY CREATOR

THE SUN
THE MOON
NOR
THE STARS
ARE A MATCH
FOR YOU
YET I
AN ANT
AMONG GIANTS
VIOLATE
CHALLENGE
AND
CURSE
YOUR LAWS
I WOULD CHANGE
IF I COULD
I GIVE YOU MY WORD
IN RETURN
I
ASK
FOR YOUR LOVE

LAST TRIP

THE TREES ARE GREEN
THE SKY IS BLUE
THE SUN IS SHINING
HAIR TOSSED
BY THE BLOWING WIND
TRAFFIC LIGHT STILL SHINING
PEOPLE HAVE NOT STOPPED
LAUGHING
AS
THE DEAD BODY
IS TAKEN
TO ITS GRAVE

REFLECTIONS

ON A SUNNY SUMMER DAY
WHEN THE TREES ARE FULL
AND
THE GRASS IS GREEN
THERE
IS NO NEED TO WORRY
OF DISHARMONY
I SIT
WATCH CHILDREN PLAY
YOUNG MINDS
SO INNOCENT SO FREE
THEY WORRY NOT WHAT
PEOPLE SAY
AH AH BUT
SUNNY DAYS
GIVE WAY
TO COLD AND BARREN DAYS
EMOTIONS FLY
LIKE LEAVES' HAPHAZARD WAY
IF CHILDREN COULD
BY CHANCE
REMAIN THE SAME
NOT CHANGE
ALWAYS
ACT IN PEACE
AS THEY DO NOW

TIME HOWEVER
WILL STAIN AND WARP
THEIR VIEWS
THEY'LL GROW UP
LIKE ME AND YOU
HOPE
FOR A NEW TOMORROW CANNOT BE
I SIT
WATCH CHILDREN PLAY
THINK OF DEATH AND
LOOK AWAY

THOUGHT # 20

A TREE STANDS
ALONE
A LEAF FALLS
ETERNITY
THE WORLD LOOKS
BUT DOES NOT SEE
A LEAF FALLS
ETERNITY
LIFE IS MOTION
NOT UNDISTURBED
A LEAF FALLS
ETERNITY
DEATH IS ETERNITY
ETERNITY IS DEATH
A TREE STANDS
ALONE
A LEAF FALLS
A BABY
IS NEW BORN

DESPERATION

WITH ONE EYE OPEN
FEET FIRM UPON THE GROUND
NO TIME TO STOP
LOOK AROUND
CLOCK TICKING TIME AWAY
THE SUN REFUSED TO SHINE
WITH ONE EYE OPEN
EMOTIONS WELL IN CONTROL
THE ROAD WAS LONG
NOW IT IS SHORT
IT WONT BE LONG
BEFORE YEARS FIRST STORM
WITH ONE EYE OPEN
MY MIND WILL KNOW IT IS TIME
HOW SMALL IS A SECOND
THE LAST FEW ARE
TOO SHORT TO KNOW

THE WORLD

HARD AND CRUEL
LOVED AND CHERISHED
BY
THOSE WHO SEE HER
AS AN END
THERE MUST BE
A BETTER PLACE
HALF AS HARD TWICE AS SWEET
FOR THOSE WHO SEE
BEYOND THE END

ONCE YOUNG

LOOK
AT THE CHILDREN PLAY
STOP
DON'T LOOK AWAY
ONCE AMONG
NOW YOU DON'T BELONG
LOOK
AT THE CHILDREN PLAY
STOP
DON'T LOOK AWAY
TIME WAS
NOW IS GONE
LOOK
AT THE CHILDREN PLAY
STOP
DON'T LOOK AWAY
TEARS
COMING DOWN YOUR CHEEK
TIME WILL NOT
LET
ITSELF REPEAT

THE MAN

YOU
ALWAYS KNOW WHICH
WAY THE WIND BLOWS
YOU
ALWAYS WANT TO RUN
THE SHOW
ME
I AM A MAN
WHO
DOES NOT UNDERSTAND
WHY THE SAND IS SHIFTING
WHEN
I LOOK THROUGH MY WINDOW
IF I OPEN MY DOOR I SEE MANY PEOPLE
CONFUSED
THEY DO NOT KNOW WHICH WAY TO GO
YOU
AND YOUR ALMIGHTY POWER
CALL THEM
YOU
WILL BE THE MAN OF THE HOUR
THEIR MIGHTY HERO
THE TIME WILL COME
WHEN
THEY WILL AWAKE FIND YOU
TO BE A FRANKENSTEIN
GO
MY FRIEND
YOU
WISH TO BE THE MAN
I HOPE YOU UNDERSTAND
WHY
I AM
LEAVING THIS LAND

30

PREGNANT LADY PLAYING POKER
WITH HER FINE GENTLEMEN
LONG HAIR MAN WITH THE SAFETY SIGN
SAYING REPENT REPENT
YOU DON'T HAVE TIME
HOWLING SIRENS
THUNDER HAS STRUCK THE NIGHT
CAN'T SAY
I THINK THERE'S TWO INSIDE
TWO BIT GIRL
I WONDER IF YOU ARE ALIVE
FLASHING NEON SIGN
CAN ALMOST BLOW YOUR MIND
SMELLY STINKING SMELL OF BEER
FAST WOMEN WITH STUFF TO SELL
ONE MILLION ANTS
WITH NO DESTINATION
I AM TRYING TO UNDERSTAND
WHAT PART IS MINE
PREGNANT LADY PLAYING POKER
I HOPE YOU UNDERSTAND
I HOLD THE JOKER
REPENT REPENT
THE WORLD WILL END TODAY
SMILING GIRL
TAKE ME TO THE PROMISE LAND

MAN # 10

WHAT MAY HE BE
IS HE AN ANIMAL
WILD OR TAME
A CREATURE
WITH OR WITHOUT SOUL
IN THESE TIMES
HOW
CAN ONE TELL

INFINITY # 10

HOW GREAT MAY IT BE
INFINITY
IS GREATNESS
INFINITY
IS SMALLNESS
MAN
IS FINITE
SO
HOW CAN HE SEE
WHAT
INFINITY MAY BE

GOODBYE

SOFT WIND BLOWING
IN THE DIRECTION OF HOME
TELL MY PEOPLE
WHERE MY HEART BELONGS
NOT LONG AGO
IN THESE DISTANT SHORES
FACING THE WIND
MY HEART LONGED FOR HOME
SOFT WIND BLOWING
IN THE DIRECTION OF HOME
TELL MY PEOPLE
I WILL SOON BE HOME
I AM NOW SEEING
MY LAST SUNDOWN
SOFT WIND BLOWING
IN THE DIRECTION OF HOME
TELL MY PEOPLE
I WISH
I DID NOT HAVE TO GO
SOFT WIND BLOWING
CARRY ME HOME
TAKE MY SOUL
BACK
TO WHERE IT BELONGS

BLACK SNAKE

IN THE GARDEN ONE DAY
I SAW A SNAKE
AMONG THE FLOWERS
CRAWLING
UGLY THING
UPON THE GROUND
UGLY BLACK THING
UPON THE GROUND
A GOOD CHRISTIAN
PROTECTING THAT
WHICH IS GOOD
I RAN
FETCHED MY WEAPON
SO ALL COULD SEE
I TOO
LOVE GOOD AND BEAUTY
IN MY HASTE TO DO MY DUTY
I FAILED TOO SEE
THE FLOWERS DESTROYED
WHILE IN MY RAGE

A MEMORY

A MEMORY OF A GIRL
FROM TIME PAST
THE SOUND OF YOUR NAME
THE SMELL IN THE AIR
HAS ONCE MORE
GIVEN JOY
FOR A MOMENT
I COULD SEE YOU
I COULD SMELL YOU
I COULD TOUCH YOU
A PLEASANT JOLT
TO MY SOUL
IF
SOMEWAY SOMEHOW
I COULD LET YOU KNOW
YOU ARE A GOOD MEMORY

THE MIND

THIS THING
YOU CALL MY MIND
IS BUT A JOKE
A TOY
TO BE ENTERTAINED
WITH SUGAR CANDY
MOLDED AND RECREATED
BY A SICK SOCIETY
TAKE ME
TO THE WORLD OUTSIDE
YOU WILL SEE
THERE IS NOTHING TO HIDE
FALSE IDEAS
STANDING USELESS
AGAINST A RUNNING TIDE
THERE IS NO HOPE
THE BOMB IS A REALITY
TELL THAT TO SOCIETY
FALSE PRETENTIONS
YOU CANNOT HIDE

© copyright 2010 Jesse Carreon

THE POET

I THINK MYSELF A POET
A GENIUS UNKNOWN TO THE WORLD
I THINK MYSELF A POET
A GENIUS MAYBE CONFUSED
I THINK MYSELF A POET
A GENIUS BY MY ACCOUNTING
I THINK MYSELF A POET
A GENIUS YES I AM SURE
MY WORDS
WILL ONE DAY BE IN PRINT
IF YOU ARE A GENIUS
YOU NEED TO BE KNOWN
THE PEACOCK PLUM
WILL BE PUT TO SHAME
WHEN I DRESS

SUN # 152

HEY SUN
UP SO HIGH
DIE
GO ON BYE
FOR ALL
THE GOOD AND WARMTH
YOU BROUGHT
I WILL GIVE YOU
NAUGHT
I
CLAIM THE DARK
WHERE
HOPE IS GONE
MY FROZEN
SOUL
CARES NO MORE
TAKE AWAY
FALSE RAYS
OF HOPE
LET ME BE
WITH MY
MISERY

A HUMBLE CHRISTIAN
(We take Christ for granted)

YES I AM
LORD ALMIGHTY MAKER OF MAN
TAKE ME TO THE PROMISE LAND
ONE SO PURE AND TRUE OF HEART
IS WORTHY FROM THIS WORLD DEPART
LORD ALMIGHTY I DO CRY
YOU ARE THE APPLE OF MY EYE
ONE SO PURE AND FREE OF SIN
YOU COULD NEVER MAKE AGAIN
IF I HAD LIVED WAY BACK THEN
I WOULD HAVE GIVEN YOU
A HELPING HAND
UNLIKE OTHERS I DO NOT SIN
BUT
WITH YOU WALK HAND IN HAND

SUMMER THUNDERSTORM

IT ROSE HIGH
50,000
MENACING
A SNAKE ABOUT TO STRIKE
FEET
TWA FLIGHT 202
WAS DIVERTED
HE SAT BY THE WINDOW
HE COULD SEE
THE UGLY CLOUD
A DARK FINGER
SILHOUETTED
AGAINST THE CLEAR SKY
A SUMMERTIME THUNDERHEAD
OR
MORE COMMONLY DESCRIBED
BY THE TV WEATHER MAN
AS
A LOCAL SEVERE STORM
SWEAT BEADS WERE FALLING
FROM HIS EYEBROWS
ROLLING DOWN
DOWN HIS CHEEKS
TEN TWENTY YEARS OF FRUSTRATION
NEXT TO THE COLD GLASS OF MILK
WAS A
GUN
THE WIND WAS BLOWING
SWIRLING
ELECTRICITY COULD BE
SMELLED
A CAGED ANIMAL ABOUT TO BREAK FREE
HE HAD
YET

TO LOAD THE GUN
AS A PRECAUTION
HE HAD STORED FIVE LIVE SHELLS
IN THE ICE BOX
KILLING WAS NOT A SOLUTION
A CONCLUSION
REACHED AFTER MANY HOURS
OF CLEAR THOUGHT
YES
AT BEST
HE WOULD COME IN LAST
NOT A DETERRENCE
NOT A DIFFERENCE
LIFE WAS THE SAME
50,000 FEET ABOVE
A SMILING FACE
CALLED OUT
COFFEE TEA OR MILK
SOME WIN SOME LOSE

BACKDOOR

STEPPED OUT THE BACKDOOR
LOOK AT CREATION
STOP
WAIT A MINUTE
STOP
SON
PUT DOWN THE GUN
TOOK A STROLL
LATE ONE NIGHT
THE RAIN HAD COOLED THE SUN HOT RAYS
TRAPPED IN CONCRETE AND STEEL
STARS TREES AND
QUIET SOUNDS OF THE NIGHT
A TRANQUILIZER
ON HOT SUMMER NIGHTS
AN UNNATURAL SOUND
MIDWAY MY STROLL
ANGRY UNKIND WORDS
AN ANGRY FACE
A TORMENTED SOUL
IN ANGER HE SCREAMED
IT IS NOT FAIR
A GUN POINTED AT A FACE
ERASES ALL THOUGHT
IN DEFENSE I CRIED

STOP
STOP SON
PUT THE GUN DOWN
BANG BANG
A DEADLY SOUND
HOT DAY OR NIGHT
COLD DAY OR NIGHT
NOTHING
A DEAD SOUND
THE BRAIN HEARS
A LAST WORD
A DRY
SORRY

60

TAKE MY HAND
WALK WITH ME
INTO TOMORROW
WHERE TOMORROW'S
NEW TRICKS
WE WILL SEE
"SAY" SAID THE MAN TO THE CAT
"TELL ME WHERE CAN IT BE
THIS PLACE
A PLACE WHERE MY GIRL AND I
ALWAYS TOGETHER BE"
"WHY"
SAID THE CAT TO THE MAN
THE CAT DID SAY
"SEE YONDER UGLY THINGS
HANGING BY THE TREE
THEY TOO WERE SEARCHING
FOR THE THINGS YOU ASK OF ME"
FROM BEHIND
TIME CRIED
"WHAT WHAT"
SAID TIME TO THE CAT
THE CAT REPLIED
"JUST ANOTHER DAY
FOR FOOLS AND THEIR DREAMS"
TIME CRIED OUT TO THE MAN
"USE ME WISELY YOU WILL NOT LIVE
FOREVER"

61

COME WITH ME TO
TO MY HOUSE IN THE SKY
SIT AT MY WINDOW
WATCH THE STARS GO BY
FEEL THE SOFT WIND
THE LOVE RHYTHM
OF INFINITY AND THE FINITE
TOGETHER
THEY PLAY
MAKE LOVE ALL NIGHT
SEE THE PLAYGROUND
OF THE LONG LOST gods
INTRIGUED WITH THEIR GAMES
HAVE LOST ALL SENSE OF REALITY
MANY COLORS PLAYING
IN A SEA OF LIGHT
ENDLESS REALITY ROAMING FREE
IT AWAITS FOR YOU AND ME
HUMAN WISHES IT CAN ACQUIRE
IF IT SO DESIRED
POOR SAMSON DELILAH A DREAM
STUPID ACTS
OF MAN GO HAND IN HAND
NOW THEY
LIE IN A HEAP
CALLED DEATH

200

THERE IS NAUGHT
AT THE END OF THE LINE
NOTHING
BUT
A HANDFUL OF TIME
AND
THE DREAMS OF MANY FOOLS
WAITING IN LINE
WAITING TO BE CALLED
IN VAIN
ONCE AGAIN

IT

FOR WANT OF A BETTER WORD
I WILL CALL YOU
IT
I HAVE CREATED GOOD
I HAVE CREATED EVIL
I WILL CALL YOU
IT
ONCE
ONCE I GAVE YOU A NAME
MAN
THAT WAS A LONG TIME AGO
I CREATED YOU
GAVE YOU INTELLIGENCE
EVEN A PERFECT
GOD
CAN CREATE AN ABERRATION
NOW
I WILL CALL YOU
IT
YOU HAVE TAKEN
ALL MY CREATIONS
MADE THEM A JOKE

MY TREES
MY WATER
NATURE
POWER
INTELLIGENCE
ALL PART OF YOU
YOU HAVE
ABUSED AND MISUSED
NOW
ON KNEES YOU ASK
FORGIVENESS
I WILL CALL YOU
IT
FROM NOW TIL
THE END OF ETERNITY
YOU WERE GIVEN ONE CHANCE
THAT IS NOW
HISTORY

A FRAUD

I APOLOGIZE
TO MY FRIENDS
TO ONE AND ALL
YOU SEE
I AM A FRAUD
YOU SEE THE SHELL
NOT THE ONE
DEEP WITHIN MY
CONSCIENCE
THE ME
WHO CRIES
WHEN I SEE
    POLLUTED WATER
    MOTHER EARTH SCARRED AND RAPED
    FOR JUSTICE
    FOR HUMANITY
    FOR HUMILITY
    FOR LOVE
YES
I AM A FRAUD
ADDICTED TOO
THE GOOD LIFE
    CARS
    WOMEN
    MONEY
    CLOTHES
    WEALTH
    SOCIAL STANDING
ALL TRAPPINGS
FOR
AN EMPTY SHELL
I AM ADDICTED
I AM A FRAUD

© copyright 2010 Jesse Carreon

101

THE SPRING SKY
CRYING TEARS
MOTHER EARTH
IS TRYING HARD TOO
HIDE
INSIDE
AWAITING THE NIGHT
SIT I
ROACHES CRAWLING DOWN A WALL
TRYING HARD NOT TO FALL
SWEET AROMA
FROM THE NEXT DOOR ROOM
LOVE SOUNDS
LOW WHISPERS
A LAUGH A SIGH AN UHMM
LOVERS
MORE
A WHISPER THAN SOUND
FROM AFAR
LAUGHING CHILDREN
SOUND
OF WORKING PEOPLE
HAPPY NOISES
ALL
    EMPHASIZE MORE
MY GLOOM
IN MY EMPTY ROOM
I WRITE A SONG
NEVER TO BE SUNG
A GENIUS
HIDDEN
BY MOTHER EARTH

KAILA AND GRANDFATHER

DARK CLOUDS
UGLY FINGERS RISING HIGH
INTO THE SKY
FARAWAY NEAR THE HORIZON
THE COLOR BLUE
CAUGHT THE CORNER OF MY EYE
A BEE
SUCKING SWEET NECTAR
FROM A FLOWER
AH LIFE CONTINUES
A MOMENT IN TIME
A SAFE NET
GRANDFATHER VIGILANT
SURROUNDS
KAILA
A CHILD
A GRANDCHILD
AH LIFE CONTINUES
FORGOTTEN LURKING
DEEP IN MEMORY
LIFE'S DANGERS
HELD AT BAY
SHEER WILLPOWER
A MIGHTY TOOL
THIS MOMENT ENJOYED
LAUGHTER
A HAPPY FACE
A SMILING FACE
A CAREFREE CHILD
RUNNING
HITHER AND THITHER
LIKE A BEE
SUCKING NECTAR
FROM LIFE

LAUGHING

WHILE THE NIGHT HIDES THE DAY
YOU KNOW
IT IS OUR TIME TO PLAY
YOU MUST REALIZE
LIFE
IS A COMPROMISE
BETWEEN YOU AND HE
WHO
LETS THE DAY ARISE
YOU GOT NOTHING TO SHOW
IF YOU DO NOT LET GO
AND
EXPLORE THE OTHER SIDE
OF YOUR FANTASIES

UNTITLED

A MOMENT IN TIME
WHEN YOUR HEART MET MINE
HAPPINESS I HAD NOT KNOWN
TILL YOUR LOVE SET ME AGLOW
A MOMENT IN TIME
BELONGING
TO YOU AND I
THE SKY IS BLUER
THE TREES GREENER
THE WORLD IS BRIGHTER
A MOMENT IN TIME

SAD TEARS

NO MATTER HOW HARD
I SHUT MY EYES
I STILL FEEL WARM TEARS
FALLING
I TOOK TIME
I SPOKE TO THE
SUN
MOON
STARS
AS A LAST RESORT
THE EARTH
IT IS NOT A FRIEND
NOR
A LOST LOVE
I SEARCH FOR TRUTH
THERE IS A VOID
A VOID IN MY SOUL
SOMETHING WITHIN
IS DYING
I WILL
SEARCH SEARCH
SOMEDAY
THE ANSWER WILL BE

102

ETERNITY IS FULL
OF DREAMS AND TIME
I AM PART OF ETERNITY
A SMALL PART
I HAVE SEEN
WHAT BECOMES OF DREAMERS
HE
WHO SAYS NAY NAY
THERE IS A BETTER WAY
HE
WHO TAKES THE ROUGHER PATH
HE
WHO GAMBLES
LOVE HAPPINESS AND SOUL
ON A DREAM
CALLED HIS OWN

DARKNESS

DARKNESS
A WELCOME STRANGER
THERE IS A THRILL
IN THE DANGER
NOT KNOWING
WHAT THE NIGHT MAY BRING
AND IF
I NEVER GET TO SEE THE LIGHT
AGAIN
I WILL
TAKE THE WHOLE JOKE
LIGHTLY

#105

LOOK
SEE ME
I SIT DREAMING
DREAMING OF A WORLD
WHERE
AMONG THE FLOWERS AND TREES
THE SKY AND SEAS
MAN
OF PEACE AND GOODWILL
MAY BE FOUND
LOOK
SEE ME
YOU CAN TELL
BY THE LOOK ON MY FACE
I KNOW
MY DREAM IS JUST A DREAM

REMEMBRANCE

A TIME LOST LONG AGO
THE DYING SUN RAYS REFLECTING OFF
A GOLDEN CRUCIFIX
HANGING HIGH ON A ALTAR
DANCING AS BLOBS OF DIFFERENT COLORS
ON A WELL WORN FLOOR
CANDLES VIGILS OF COLORS
WHITE RED AND BLUE
ALL IN SILENT PRAYER
FOR DEAD SOULS
FOR A QUARTER A SINNER
GETS A SECOND CHANCE AT HEAVEN
I GUESS THE RICH ARE BLESSED
IN MORE WAYS THAN ONE
MERCY ON THE POOR
THE DING DONG ECHOES OF A BELL
STILL RINGS SOFTLY IN MY EAR
TEN MINUTES TO VESPERS
TIME
TO THANK GOD FOR A GIVEN DAY
NOT MANY ARE BLESSED
SO IT SEEMS
TWO LADIES AND AN OLD MAN
THE AVERAGE
NO ONE ELSE
EXCEPT ME AND THE PRIEST
LONELY EERIER REFRAINS OF A PRAYER OFFERED
IN THANKSGIVING
ECHOING
INSIDE AN OLD AND NEAR EMPTY CHURCH
THE HUSTLE AND BUSTLE OF LIFE
DEMAND A LARGE PRICE
SELF INDULGENCE
IS AN UGLY BEAST
GOD
MUST BE PATIENT

801

TIME IS INFINITE
YES NO
MAYBE SO
WHO KNOWS
THE DOG CHASING THE TAIL
MAN MADE
LAWS AND IDEAS
CONSTANT AS
CHANGING TIME
MANKIND
ASKING TO BE A god
ASKING TO CONVERSE WITH GOD
LOOKING WITH CLOSED EYES
INFINITY = INFINITY
ARROGANCE IS NOT DEAD

TRUST

I DO NOT KNOW
WHY WHY
I
TRUST TRUST
MAN
CLOUDS STARS LIFE
ALL
A
TEMPORARY EXISTENCE
WHITE TURNED TO GRAY
BLACK TURNED TO WHITE
OPAQUE
TRUTH NAKED STANDING ALONE
WHIPPED
BY THE WHIMS OF MAN'S
AMBITION POWER GREED FAME
IN MAN I TRUST
WHY WHY
ABSURD
PLACE MY TRUST
ON MANKIND
A FINE MIST
ON THE SEA OF TIME

DALLAS 1957 STORM

THE FLOOR OF THE SEMINARY SHOOK
JUST A LITTLE
AIR PRESSURE PRESSING THE BUILDING
SHOUTS FROM FELLOW SEMINARIANS
LOOK LOOK
OUT THE WALL'S LONG WINDOWS
MAYBE TWO MILES AWAY
A SINGLE BLACK CLOUD
A FINGER ETCHING THE EARTH
SLOWLY THE FINGER MOVED
TORNADO TORNADO SOMEONE SHOUTED
WHAT'S THE EXCITEMENT
IGNORANCE IS BLISS
I STOOD CAPTURED
BY A WONDER I HAD NOT SEEN
EXCITEMENT AND TENSION BY THOSE
WHO KNEW
AWAY FROM THE WINDOWS
DOWN TO THE BASEMENT
HURRY HURRY MOVE MOVE
SUCH A WONDROUS SIGHT
THAT DARK FIGURE
FATHER JEROME
OUR MENTOR BROKE MY SPELL
WE ARE IN DANGER WE ARE IN DANGER
I WAS BLIND I COULD NOT SEE
DANGER DANGER WHERE WHERE
NOT
FROM A BLACK CLOUD WITH A FINGER

THE DALLAS TORNADO IN 1957 KILLED
A MEMORY OF HORROR TO MANY
LOST LIVES LOST DREAMS
A PAIN NEVER TO BE FORGOTTEN
I STILL REMEMBER
THE BEAUTY AND WONDER
MOTHER NATURE STRUTTING HER STUFF
MANKIND HELPLESS

????

GOD NO GOD
DEATH PERMANENT
A VOID
AN
AFTER LIFE
REINCARNATION
A SECOND COMING
SOME
CLAIM EACH
I
HEAR MANY VOICES
ALL
CLAIMING TRUTH
ASTRONOMY PHYSICS AND MATHEMATICS
LANGUAGES OF GOD
FLASHLIGHTS
LOOKING FOR THE TRUTH
THE MOMENT OF CREATION
THE BIG BANG
SOLAR WIND
MAJESTIC CLOUDS
OF WHAT
POWER ENERGY
YOU SEEN THE PICTURES
HUGE COLUMNS OF????

THANKS MR. HUBBLE
LAWS OF CHEMISTRY
LAWS OF LAW
LAWS OF NATURE
LAWS OF MAN
WHAT APPLIES
TWO PROBLEMS
THE BIG GETS BIGGER
THE SMALL GETS SMALLER
EACH SAY MAYBE
ANSWER NOT CLEAR
TRUTH THE CARROT
$E=MC^2$
UNIFIED THEORY
AN ANSWER
AN ANSWER
THE CARROT
ALWAYS AHEAD

THE CHRIST

HE WAS BORN
A HUMAN
FLESH
BLOOD
BONE
NOT UNLIKE YOU OR I
A SAVIOR
SO HE SAID
I AM WHO I AM
SON OF GOD
A SAVIOR
YOU SWINE
WHIPPED CRUCIFIED
CROWNED WITH THORNS
A KING YOUR KING
KING OF JEWS
YES I AM
DEAD DEAD DEAD
HA
A GOD
BORN HUMAN
SELF SERVING
SELF RIGHTEOUS

PRIDEFUL
PRESUMPTUOUS
A HUMAN BORN
YET A GOD
SON OF GOD
NO HELP NO HELP
GODS DO NOT DIE
ON A CROSS
HARD HARD TRUTHS
A FRAUD
A DARK LIGHT
AN ABERRATION
NOT A SAVIOR
BORN HUMAN
FLESH BLOOD AND BONE
NOT A GOD
SO WE HOPE

UNCLEAR SKY

THE SUN LOOMS
AS STRINGS
OF RED AND YELLOW
RAYS OF LIGHT
ILLUMINATING
A DARKENED AND UGLY SKY
FALLING DOWN
NEAR THE HORIZON
THE DARK SILHOUETTE
OF A NAKED TREE
BRIGHT FINGERS OF LIGHTNING
HAPHAZARD SCARS
ACROSS THE EVENING
SKY
MELANCHOLY
A SWEET DRINK
FOR AN ALREADY
BEATEN SOUL
HOPE
LIKE THE SUN RAYS
A DISAPPEARING ACT
A DARK CLOUD
MUCH TOO BIG
ENGULFING
STIFLING
BURDENSOME
AND
IN THE FAR DISTANCE
A SPECK OF LIGHT
A MEMORY
A RECOLLECTION
A NAME
REMEMBERED
I AM WHO I AM

FOR MY WIFE

A DRY CACTUS
MORE THE COLOR OF SAND
THE GREEN IS HARD TO SEE
A SPRIG
OUT IN THE MIDDLE
OF THE CHISOS MOUNTAINS
IN WEST TEXAS
THE PERSONALITY OF A 2x4
A GOOD DESCRIPTION OF
MY PERSON
NOT BLESSED
WITH LOOKS OR PERSONALITY
IN CONTRAST
A RED ROSE
A BEAUTY TO THE EYE
RED
DEEP AS THE COLOR OF BLOOD
PEDESTALS
SOFT AS COTTON
CLASS AMONG CLASS
A BEAUTY
DESERVING A PLACE
HIGHER
ON THE ALTAR OF LIFE
MY WIFE

LOVE # 2

IT FLOWS
IN AND OUT
AN INTANGIBLE MESS
TOUCHING
HERE AND THERE
AND LIKE
THE GOOD INTENTIONS OF MAN
IT IS VERY HARD
TO UNDERSTAND

QUESTION

I LOOK AT THE SUN
A WONDER
I SEE THE MOUNTAINS
MAJESTIC
AGAINST THE BLUE SKY
I SEE MANY WONDERS
IN THIS WORLD
YET
BLIND I AM TO YOU
A PIERCED BODY
FLOGGED AND BEATEN
HANGING
ON A WOODEN CROSS
A BLIND MAN
HAS
BETTER SIGHT THAN I

LOST FOR WORDS

TRY TRY
WRITE
ABOUT WHAT
WRITE
ABOUT WHAT
MY BRAIN IS DRY DRY
AS A LAKE ON A SUMMER DROUGHT
TWIGS
DRY KINDLE
LOST MEMORIES
LOST DREAMS
WORDS AND IDEAS
WELL HIDDEN
DEEP WITHIN A DRY WELL
DUG
ONCE TOO OFTEN
A LABOR NOT EASY
ALL A QUARRY OF GRANITE
COME BACK COME BACK
LOST FRIEND
I LONG FOR YOUR FRIENDSHIP
AND GENEROSITY
SHINE YOUR LIGHT ONCE MORE
HONOR ME WITH YOUR PRESENCE
WRITE WRITE
I NEED IDEAS
I NEED IDEAS

TO A POLLUTED LAKE

I PITY YOU
MRS. LAKE
YOUR BEAUTY
DESTROYED BY A SCUM
CALLED MAN
ONCE YOU WERE A BEAUTY
A MIRROR TO ALL
A CANVAS FOR THE CLOUDS
IN THE SKY
A SALVE FOR THE SOUL
A RHAPSODY FOR LOVERS
A PLAYGROUND FOR MANY
NOW
LIKE A WOUNDED ANIMAL
YOU HAVE NONE
TO CARE OR MEND YOUR WOUNDS
IN TIME YOU WILL DIE
GOODBYE MY FRIEND
GOODBYE

WAXAHACHIE

MORE AN APPARITION
A SIGHTING
HIDDEN
BEHIND A MIST OF FOG
MORE A THOUGHT
NOT FACT
THE LIPS
THE EYES
A SMILE
THE WALK
THE TALK
A MEMORY
PLUCKED
FROM THE HEAP OF ABANDON FORGOTTEN
DEAD DREAMS AND LOST THOUGHTS
A GLASS OF SPILLED WATER
IN THE MIDDLE OF THE HOT SAHARA
NOT THE EFFECT
RATHER THE ACTION
A JINGLE OF THE ELECTRONS
IN THE MEMORY SECTION
OF THE BRAIN
A SWEET MEMORY EVER SO GENTLE
A BREEZE
OF A TIME LONG LOST
A BEAUTIFUL SMILE
A SOFT
I LOVE YOU
A FORGOTTEN LOVE

HOPE

SOMEPLACE
DOWN THE ROAD OF CREATION
WHERE FAITH FIRST HAD ITS ORDINATION
HOPE WAITING TO BE FOUND
A HELPING HAND FOR A NEWBORN BABY
MAYBE
A NEW BIRTH
NEW BLOOD
FOR MOTHER EARTH
AROUND THE CORNER FROM THE EDGE OF TIME
A DEAD SOUL CRIES FOR ANOTHER TRY
TOMORROW CANNOT BE WITHOUT HOPE
FOR YOU OR ME
FREE WE MUST BE OR ELSE WE DIE
BLIND WE ARE AND BLIND WE SEE
THIS WORLD IS IN TROUBLE
OR IS IT JUST ME
A NEWBORN THERE MAY BE HOPE
HAND IN HAND WORKING TOGETHER
SOCIETY NEED NOT UNDERSTAND
AROUND THE CORNER FROM THE EDGE OF TIME
A DEAD SOUL CRIES FOR ANOTHER TRY
YOU HAD YOUR CHANCE YOU COULD NOT SEE
YOU CLAIMED LIFE AND ITS MISERIES
YOU COULD NOT UNDERSTAND
THE LIFE YOU LIVED WAS CHEAP AND NO GOOD
LOOK SEE THE WORLD IS IN DISGUISE
SOLD OUT TO THE HIGHEST PRICE
YOU LIVED YOUR LIVE ALL IN VAIN
A NEWBORN
A NEW BLOOD
HOPE
THERE IS TIME
MAYBE

UNTITLED

I SAW A DEAD FLOWER
MANY THOUGHTS CAME THAT HOUR
BRIGHT SUN SHINING
ALL BELOW ARE CRYING
THE COP WITH THE NIGHT STICK
SOCIETY IN CONTROL
TRUST YOUR LEADERS
STOP LOOK LISTEN
ALL BELOW ARE CRYING
I SAW A DEAD FLOWER
HEAR THE BABY CRY
SUN DO NOT FORGET
UPON THIS EARTH WE ONCE MET
CHILDREN STOP ALL THE CRYING
CAN'T YOU SEE THE SUN IS SHINING
WHILE WE ALL SIT IN OUR ROUND
COMFORTABLE CHAIRS

A WARNING

UNBORN CHILD
IF ONLY YOU COULD KEEP YOUR LIFE
WITHIN YOUR MOTHER'S WOMB
IF YOUR PROBLEMS COULD BE FEW
YOU WOULD KNOW WHAT TO DO
LIFE IS NOT A PLEASANT DREAM
STAY WITHIN
HARD DAYS LONELY NIGHTS
DO NOT THINK ALL WILL BE RIGHT
PLEASE DON'T COME OUTSIDE
IF SOMEHOW YOU COULD FEEL
THIS FEAR THAT WITHIN ME STIRS
I KNOW YOU STAY WITHIN
AND JUNK THE REST

TEACHER

A DEAD BIRD CAN'T SING
A BROKEN BELL WON'T RING
THE EMPTY MIND CAN'T COMPREHEND
THE LONELY CHILD WON'T UNDERSTAND
EMPTY PROMISES OF THINGS TO BE
WHEN HE KNOWS WELL
YOU AND ME
THE TALKERS ARE TALKING
THE DOERS ARE DOING
THE BICKERERS ARE BICKERING
THE SCHEMERS ARE SCHEMING
THE THINKERS ARE THINKING
THE DREAMERS ARE DREAMING
THE LOST ARE LOST
YOU EXPECT THEN TO UNDERSTAND
THINGS YOU DON'T KNOW
BLIND EYES CANNOT SEE
MANKIND AND HIS PRIDE
PROMISES SOON FORGOTTEN
OFFERED FREE
LEFT HANGING ON A TREE
A FORGERY AN ILLUSION
MEANWHILE
THE EMPTY MIND OF THE CHILD
IS GROWING WILD

© copyright 2010 Jesse Carreon

KAILA AT SEVEN

IF I WAS TO SAY
MY LOVE FOR YOU
IS BRIGHTER
THAN THE SUN OR THE STARS
IT WOULD BE A LIE
MY LOVE FOR YOU
STARTS DEEP PAST
MY CONSCIOUS BEING
DEEP PAST
MY EARTHLY TIES
PAST
ALL STARS AND ALL SUNS
TO THE FRONT YARD
OF THE HOUSE OF GOD
YOU
THE SECOND GENERATION
OF THE BLOOD MIXTURE
OF YOUR GRANDMOTHER AND I
THE CHAIN OF LIFE
CONTINUES
ON THE NIGHT
OF YOUR BIRTH
I LIFTED YOU UP HIGH
INTRODUCED YOU TO GOD
YOUR GRANDMOTHER
THOUGHT I WAS DANCING
I MADE
A VOW AND A PROMISE
KAILA ELDORA GIBBS
I AM YOUR GRANDFATHER
JESSE CARREON
I WILL
ALWAYS LOVE YOU

MANKIND

THE WASTELAND
CALLED HUMANITY
WITH THEIR
PRIDE AND VANITY
NO WONDER THE DESTRUCTION
NOW THEY HAVE REACHED
A JUNCTION
ONLY ONE WAY FOR THEM TO GO
OTHERWISE THEY WILL LOSE
THEIR SHOW
FIGHTING AND KILLING
ALL FOR NAUGHT
A POMPOUS PEACOCK

PR SCHEME

MAN CRIES
THERE IS
NO GOD
NONE NONE
    HE AIN'T SUPER
    FOR ALL WE KNOW
    HE MAY BE
    LIKE SANTA CLAUS
    THE CLASSIC
    PR SCHEME
AND
IN HIS VANITY
HE STRUTS
INTELLIGENTSIA

DIRT

MAN LIKE THE FLOWERS
WILL WITHER AND DIE
TIME WILL ERASE
ALL SCARS FROM
HIS STONY FACE
THE WORM WILL TAKE
ALL
RETURN HIM BACK
TO THE GROUND
IT IS THEN
MAN
WILL BE EXPOSED
AND
LIE IN DISGRACE

NO CHOICE

I CARRY QUESTIONS
THEY MUST BE ANSWERED
SOMEDAY
FOR THE TIME
I WILL BE SATISFIED
WITH THIS THING CALLED LIFE
I HAVE BEEN THROWN INTO THIS CHAMBER
WITHOUT CHOICE
I MUST DANCE THIS DANCE
I WAS THROWN DEEP WITHOUT CONCERN
GIVEN NO CHOICE I MUST SURVIVE
IT IS NOT MY GAME
IT BELONGS TO ANOTHER

PLAYTIME

WHILE
THE NIGHT HIDES THE DAY
IT IS TIME TO PLAY
YOU MUST
REALIZE LIFE IS A COMPROMISE
BETWEEN
YOU AND HE
WHO LETS DAY ARISE
YOU
GOT NOTHING TO SHOW
IF
YOU DON'T LET GO
AND
EXPLORE THE OTHER SIDE
OF YOUR FANTASIES
PAINT YOURSELF A FACE
TASTE LIFE
NEVER LET GO

104

BAD DREAM
ON A MONDAY MORNING
MY HEAD IS RUSHING
ROUND AND ROUND
MY SOUL NO PLACE
TO BE FOUND
A ONE WAY TICKET
TO THE EDGE OF TIME
BOTH
MIND AND SOUL
GONE FOREVER
BRIGHT LIGHT FLOATING BY
DON'T HIDE
I NEED A RIDE BE MY GUIDE
THERE
MY SOUL AND MIND MUST BE
AT THE EDGE OF TIME
OH OH
WHAT IS THE USE
BOTH
SOUL AND MIND ABUSED
MAY WISH
NOT TO BE FOUND
ON A MIRROR
I CAN SEE TWO OF ME
WAIT I'LL GO GET MORE
COMPANY
HELLO DARKNESS
WHAT IS YOUR NAME

A PUPPET

REFLECTIONS OF A MIRROR
SILLY LITTLE CLOWN
DANCE
DANCE
TO A TUNE HEARD ONLY BY YOU
YOU AND THAT STUPID GRIN
WHO PULLS YOUR STRINGS
WHO MAKES YOU MOVE
WHAT SECRETS DO YOU HIDE

WEAK

I HAVE OFTEN
SAID GOODBYE
MORE THAN ONCE
MORE THAN ONCE
I HAVE WALKED AWAY
YET
HERE I AM BACK AGAIN
AND
HERE I WILL BE
UNTIL THAT DAY
I KNOW IT IS COMING
YOU WILL TURN OFF
THE LIGHT
SAY
GOODBYE

DOUBT

LONELY MAN
WITH NO FACE
YOU SAY
THE WORLD IS TURNING
FAR TO FAST
PROGRESS
WILL NOT LET YOU REST
LATE AT NIGHT
YOU FIGHT YOUR DOUBTS
MORNINGS BRING
BACK YOUR SMILE
YOUR INVESTMENT STOCKS
FAR SURPASS YOUR GOAL
A WHITEWASH
FOR A TROUBLED SOUL
A FIGHT YOU FIGHT
YOU BUILD A SHRINE
OF POWER AND WEALTH
FOR NONE BUT YOU
THE EMPTY LIFE
OF A LONELY MAN
AND
SOMETIMES LATE AT NIGHT
IN DESPERATION
YOU CRY OUT WHY ME LORD

LIES

THE RAINY DAY CLOUDS
WITH THEIR UGLY FACE
WRAP
THE SKY IN A DARK EMBRACE
AND YOU
HAVE FALLEN
OFF THEIR HORSE
FACE DOWN YOU LIE
EATING DIRT
WHAT CAN YOU DO
WHAT CAN YOU SAY
TRUTHS YOU HAD EMBRACED
WITHOUT QUESTION
THEIR HOLLOW PROMISES
YOU NOW FIND
EMPTY EMPTY
ASK NO QUESTIONS
YOU ARE FIGHTING
A LOST FIGHT
IF YOU TRY TO UNDERMINE
LIES
HANDED DOWN THRU TIME
ONCE
ACCEPTED AS TRUTHS
BY YOU
ALL
IN THE NAME OF PEACE

FORGOTTEN POEMS

SOMEWHERE
IN THE BACK
CORNER OF MY MIND
WHERE THOUGHTS AND IDEAS
LIKE FLOWERS ARE GROWN
THEY LIE IN WAIT
FOR A SEARCHING LIGHT
TIME IS A TRUE ERASER
THOUGHTS AND IDEAS
WELL KEPT
LOCKED DEEP WITHIN
NEVER TO COME OUT
TO TEST THE WIND OF LIFE
NONE
SHOULD FIND COMFORT
NOTHING IS SAFE WITHIN
NO NOT
WHEN
TIME DOES ITS JOB WELL

HATE

COME WITH ME TO A PLACE
WHERE
THE DARK CLOUDS OF HATE ARE BORN
THE SUN DOES CAST A DARK LIGHT
    SOMETIMES
A PLACE NOT FAR
CAN BE ANY HOME
CAN BE ANY PEOPLE
YOUNG OR OLD
BLACK YELLOW OR WHITE
NONE ARE IMMUNE
A MOMENT IN TIME
A CHOICE
YES OR NO
YING YANG
A DECISION OF THE HEART
A COMPROMISE OF THE MIND

LAUGH

WE LAUGHED
DEEP INTO THE NIGHT
WHILE
DREAMS OF YESTERDAY
FLOATED BEFORE OUR EYES
THREE GENERATIONS
TWO SEATED ONE PLAYING
WHILE
TALES OF TIMES GONE BY
WERE TOLD
TOLD AS JOKES TO HIDE
THE PAIN AND SORROW
EXPERIENCED
ONCE AS CHILDREN
SECRET WEAKNESS
OF A FATHER OR MOTHER
ALCOHOL
ANGER
UNHAPPINESS
FAILURE
EXPLOSIONS WITHOUT WARNING
HURLING DAMNING DAGGERS
DEEP INTO YOUNG HEARTS
FEARS AND PAIN
ONCE SO DOMINANT

NOW SEEN
AS FUNNY ABERRATIONS
OF A ONCE UNTRANQUIL
FAMILY LIFE
GHOSTS
ONCE FRIGHTENING
NOW SEEN IN A DIFFERENT LIGHT
EMOTIONS AND PAINS
LONG FORGOTTEN
SURFACE ONCE AGAIN
TALES
TOLD AGAIN
NOT AS DAMNING
RECOLLECTIONS
MORE
AS A SALVE
TO SOOTHE ACHING HEARTS

ADVERTISEMENT ON TV

I AM THE DIRTY CHILD
THE ONE RUNNING WILD
DIRTY HAIR DIRTY BOOTS
YOU DON'T LIKE MY LOOKS
MY MIND IS OPEN
SO IS MY HEART
WITHIN ME THERE IS NO DOUBT
SOCIETY IS NO PLACE TO BE
TRY TRY
YOU CANNOT KEEP ME
OUT OF SIGHT
IT IS NOT MY MIND
BUT MY HEART
THAT
WON'T LET UP ITS SHOUT
A PLACE TO REST MY MIND
A PLACE TO LIVE NOT DIE
I AM THE CHILD YOU SEE
BETWEEN COMMERCIALS
ON YOUR TV

ONE SIDED CONVERSATION

GOD SPOKE TO ME
NO THUNDER NO SPLASH
A DREAM --- VERY REAL
SAID HE
I GAVE YOU THE:
    MOON
    SUN
    STARS
    GALAXIES
GREAT WONDERS OF NEAR SPACE
I LET YOU PEEK FAR INTO SPACE
YOU YET TO SCRATCH THE SURFACE
I WOULD GIVE YOU MUCH MORE
SAID HE
I GAVE YOU:
    MATHEMATICS
    PHYSICS
    CHEMISTRY
    BIOLOGY
    ENGINEERING
    LANGUAGE
    INTELLIGENCE
    DETERMINATION
ALL WONDER TOOLS FOR DISCOVERY
I HAVE SEEN THE WONDERS
YOU HAVE DEVELOPED
YOU YET TO SCRATCH THE SURFACE
I WOULD GIVE YOU MUCH MORE
SAID HE

I GAVE YOU:

    PREFERENCE OVER ALL CREATURES

    DOMINANCE OF YOUR LIFE

    A FREE WILL

    LIBERTY OF MIND AND BODY

    LOVE OR HATE YOUR CHOICE

I HAVE SEEN YOUR EFFORTS

I HAVE SEEN YOUR FAILURES

I KNOW OF YOUR STRUGGLES

I KNOW OF YOUR PAIN

YES

I GAVE YOU THESE

YOU YET TO SCRATCH THE SURFACE

SAID HE

I GAVE YOU: MY SON

    IN CHRIST MY SON

    I GAVE YOU HOPE

    I GAVE YOU LOVE

    I GAVE YOU PEACE

IN REPLY YOU

YOU

HUNG HIM ON A CROSS

KING OF KINGS

YOU YET TO SCRATCH THE SURFACE

I WOULD GIVE YOU SO MUCH MUCH MORE

A VISIT

HE WAS THE IDEAL MAN
HE OOZED
WEALTH AND FAME
POWER AND GLORY
ALL HIS
BEAUTIFUL WOMEN
POWERFUL MEN
ALL AT HIS COMMAND
HE HEARD THE COMMOTION
LONG BEFORE HE SAW
THE CROWD ON TOP OF THE HILL
ANGRY SHOUT
MINGLED WITH
CRIES OF AGONY
THE CLANG
METAL ON METAL
IN HIS MILLION DOLLAR SUIT
MINGLING AMONG RIFF RAFF
COARSE PEOPLE
IGNORANT PEOPLE
HE COULD NOT SEE
NO
THE PERFUME OF
POWER
FAME
PRIDE
TO STRONG TO STRONG
NO NO
HE MOVED TOO FAST
AND AS HE TOPPED
THE NEXT HILL
HE FAILED TO SEE
THE SILHOUETTE OF
THREE FIGURES HUNG
ONE WHO IS CALLED
KING OF KINGS

MY SAVIOR

YOUR CROSS IS HEAVY
YOUR CROSS IS HEAVY
YOUR CROSS IS HEAVY
WHY/HOW DO YOU EXPECT ME
TO CARRY
SUCH A BURDEN
SUCH A BURDEN
I SEE
I FEEL
I TASTE
I SMELL
I HEAR
ALL WINDOWS TO MY SOUL
ALL CRY
COME
COME
SHARE A WONDROUS BOUNTY
SWEET FLAVORS
A SALVE
FOR A HUNGRY BODY
A LUSCIOUS FOREST
WHERE
ALL NEEDS ARE MET
I LOOK ONCE AGAIN
I SEE YOUR PAIN
AND
ANOTHER STEP
I TAKE

THE CHRIST

I FIRST HEARD OF HE
ON MY 4TH OR 5TH YEAR
A PROMISE OF A GREAT MAN
NO
A GREAT LEADER
NO
I FIRST SAW THE CHILD OF CHRISTMAS
POORER THAN DIRT
FILTH WAS HIS BED
A BUNDLE OF LOVE
A WONDROUS CHILD
SO WAS SAID
WE SANG HIM A SONG
THIS IS MY MEMORY
LIVING DEMANDS CHOICE
GOOD OR BAD RIGHT OR WRONG
LOOK IN THE MIRROR
IT'S YOU
THE EYE CANDY OF THIS WORLD
IS ATTRACTIVE AND SWEET
THE CONSTANT CHATTER
AND
NOISE OF THE WORLD
A GOOD BLIND FOR THE SOUL
FRONT TO REAR LEFT TO RIGHT
A CIRCUMFERENCE OF A CIRCLE
IF TRACED
LIFE IS SIMPLE
HAPPINESS - FEAR
LOVE - HATE

YES
A CIRCLE IS LIFE
AROUND AND AROUND
WHERE TO STOP
HOW SOON COMES THE END
THE NEW IS OLD A LIFE PASSED
TIME THE EXECUTIONER
NONE IS SPARED
THEY CALLED HIM THE CHRIST
THEY CALLED HIM
THE SON OF GOD
A MEMORY FORGOTTEN

MEMORIES

THE MIND THEY
SAY
IS A RECORDER
SWEET DREAMS
OF A TIME PAST
A NAME
A PLACE
A PERSON
A SPECIAL PERSON
THAT
TIME HAS ERASED
BOTH
FACE AND MEMORY
YET
THE THOUGHT
REWOUND
GIVES
A SPECIAL JOY
TO A SAD AND HURTING
HEART
A FEW MOMENTS OF JOY
AN
APPETIZER FOR A MEAL
ENJOYED
A LONG TIME
AGO

JESUS CHRIST/ MESSIAH

HE WALKS
ALONE
DOWN A COUNTRY ROAD
SURROUNDED BY VEGETATION
GREEN TREES
FLOWERS OF ALL COLORS
THE ANIMAL KINGDOM
ALIGNED
ONE BY ONE
CREATION STOOD
OPENED MOUTH
IN AWE
HE
THE MAN/ THE GOD
CALLED
JESUS CHRIST
ABOVE
THE BLUE SKY AND THE BRIGHT SUN
ALL
JOINED TOGETHER IN
SILENT PRAYER
THEY ALL KNOW
THE MISSION
ONE ORDAINED BY
GOD CREATOR
ON THE HORIZON
UP AHEAD
THE CITY
A CITY FILLED
WITH ALL
STINKS PAINS AND SORROWS
KNOWN TO THE WORLD
DEATH AWAITS
AN UGLY DARK CLOUD

HANGS OVERHEAD
AS A WARNING
TO ALL
ESPECIALLY TO
HE
ENTER AT YOU OWN RISK
UP ON HIS THRONE
LUCIFER
WITH A DEVIOUS SMILE
MUMBLES
WELCOME WELCOME
YET
THE GOD MAN
CONTINUOUS
KNOWING WHAT AWAITS
IN OBEDIENCE AND GREAT LOVE
FOR
HE CARRIES A PROMISE
TO THE WORLD
BLESSED MESSIAH EMANUEL

GOODS SOLD

THERE
IS A HEAVEN AND HELL
OH REALLY
GOOD GUYS AND BAD GUYS
OH REALLY
THE DIVIDING LINE
ONE SIDE GOES TO HEAVEN (THE GOOD GUYS)
THE OTHER TO HELL (THE BAD GUYS)
ME
THINKEST
'TIS A PRODUCT
SOLD
BY THE CHURCH
TO THOSE
WHO ARE IN NEED

© copyright 2010 Jesse Carreon
(This is not Christianity, it's propaganda)

INCIDENT

MAD DOG ON THE LOOSE
OR
A MEXICAN LOOKING FOR HELP
IN AFFLUENT NORTH DALLAS AFTER 6 PM
MANY WILL CALL IT MY IMAGINATION
OTHERS
WILL SAY IT NEVER HAPPENED
BY ACCIDENT
I WAS FORCED TO SEEK HELP
ONE LATE WINTER DAY
COLD WIND CUTTING MY SKIN
GOD WISH IT WEREN'T COLD
MY PHYSICAL DISCOMFORT
WAS SOON FORGOTTEN
AFTER STOPPING AT TWO HOUSES
THE DOUBTS THE FEARS
IN PEOPLE EYES
I COULD FEEL THEIR FEAR
IT CUT DEEP IN MY HEART
IT HELPED DESTROY
THAT MYTH
PEOPLE ARE FRIENDLY IN TEXAS
OR
ASK AND YOU SHALL RECEIVE

© copyright 2010 Jesse Carreon

JOE DEAN

WAS A WEEK BEFORE CHRISTMAS
THEREABOUTS
ME AND JOE DEAN HAD SPENT MOST OF THE
MORNING
TALKING OF THE DAYS AHEAD
THE BLUE SUMMER SKY
DID LITTLE TO SUGGEST
WINTER WAS A FEW DAYS OLD
ANYWAY
SUMMER WAS A FEW MONTHS AGO
WELL
JOE DEAN SAID HE WANTED A RIFLE
HE LOVED TO GO HUNTING
JOE DEAN CALLED EARLY CHRISTMAS DAY
HE GOT HIS GUN
I WAS HAPPY FOR JOE DEAN
THE NEXT FEW YEARS JOE DEAN AND I DIDN'T SEE
MUCH OF EACH OTHER
HE LOVED TO HUNT
I DIDN'T
WHEN WE WERE BOTH 18
WE WENT OUR SEPARATE WAYS
TWO FRIENDS CANNOT REMAIN TOGETHER
FOREVER
FOR THE PAST FEW YEARS
A WEEK BEFORE CHRISTMAS

I RECALLED MY FRIEND JOE DEAN
JOE DEAN AND I
SHARED SOME HEARTFELT MOMENTS
I STILL KEEP SECRETS WE SHARED
I SAW JOE DEAN'S MOTHER THE OTHER DAY
TOLD ME
JOE DEAN HAD A BOY
ABOUT THE SAME AGE AS MINE
I WISH NEVER MIND
JOE DEAN AND I WERE GOOD FRIENDS
NOW
HE LIVES HIS LIFE
AND
I MINE

DEAD BIRD

A DEAD BIRD CANNOT SING
A BROKEN BELL WILL NOT RING
THE EMPTY MIND CANNOT COMPREHEND
A LONELY CHILD WILL NOT UNDERSTAND
PROMISES OF THINGS TO BE
THE DEAD BIRD SOON COVERED
BY THE WINTER STORM
THE SILENT BELL SOON TO BE GONE
YOU EXPECT A CHILD TO COMPREHEND
THINGS
YOU DO NOT UNDERSTAND
PROMISES
NEVER MEANT TO BE
ARE SOON FORGOTTEN
LEFT
HANGING ON A TREE
THE EMPTY MIND OF THE LONELY
CHILD
MEANWHILE IS GOING WILD

SQUIRREL

I SAW A SQUIRREL CLIMB A TREE
IT BROUGHT MEMORIES
BACK TO ME
OF
A TIME
LOST
NOT LONG AGO
THOSE GOOD YOUNG DAYS
WHEN MOTHER WOULD SAY
COME IN SON
IT'S LATE DAY
TOGETHER WE SIT TO HAVE OUR MEAL
MY PARENTS BROTHER SISTERS AND ME
TOGETHER WE KEPT GUARD
LESS A SHOOTING STAR UNKNOWING GO BY
MY PARENTS BROTHER SISTERS AND ME
TOGETHER WE HAVE GROWN OLD
AND
LIKE THE LEAVES ON A LATE AUTUMN DAY
WILL SOON FALL
MY PARENTS BROTHER SISTERS AND ME

© copyright 2010 Jesse Carreon

USELESS THOUGHTS ON A RAINY DAY

WHAT IF: NIGHT WAS DAY
WHAT IF: WHITE WAS BLACK
WHAT IF: TOMORROW WAS TODAY
WHAT IF: WRONG WAS RIGHT
WHAT IF: HATE WAS LOVE
WHAT IF: THERE WAS NO PAIN NOR SORROW
WHAT IF: MAN LOVED MAN

YOU

SEE
HOW THE FLOWERS BLOOM
THEY
COULD BE YOU AND I
PRETTY COLORS GOING PAST MY MIND
I FEEL MYSELF CARRIED TO THE EDGE OF TIME
BLUE IS HOW I FEEL WHEN I DON'T SEE YOU
WHITE IS FOR THE PURE OF HEART
RED IS FOR THE BRAVE AND STRONG
VIOLET IS FOR THE PAMPERED
A TASTE TOO STRONG
SEE ALL THE FLOWERS GLOW
ARTIFICIAL EYE CANDY
NOT HALF
THE BEAUTY I SEE IN YOU

THE SAD CASE OF MR. JAY SEE

HE WAS BORN IN A COUNTRY WHICH
FOR THE BETTER PART WAS NOT HIS OWN
FROM THE START HE KNEW
THIS WORLD HIS HOME WAS AN ENEMY
FROM EARLY LIFE HE GAVE FREE ADVICE
LOVE ONE ANOTHER
TURN THE OTHER CHEEK
FORGIVE YOUR ENEMIES
SOUNDS GOOD TO ME
YOUNG JAY SEE ALL COULD SEE
WOULD GO FAR IN THIS LIFE
HE AND HIS GANG OF TWELVE
WOULD GO FAR
YES
A GOOD COMMODITY HAD HE
CHEAP TOO
FREE
INTERNAL AUDITS AND FALSE ADVERTISING
UNFAIR PRACTICES
WAS THE CALL
FROM THOSE IN POWER
A DANGER TO SOCIETY
AN UNBALANCING OF THE POWER STRUCTURE
A DREAMER
A PLAYER OF MIRRORS
NOTHING ELSE
HOT AIR
ON A FRIDAY HE WAS TAKEN FOR A RIDE
DISPLAYED
SO ALL COULD SEE
HE WAS JUST ANOTHER HUMAN
A MADMAN
NOTHING ELSE

DABOO/DAWOO

I WILL ANSWER TO EITHER
MY GRANDDAUGHTER'S
INTERPRETATION OF GRANDFATHER
DABOO/DAWOO
A BIG GRIN
A SMILING FACE
SPARKLING EYES
OPEN ARMS SHE RUSHES
A BIG EMBRACE
UNCOMPROMISED LOVE
A GOLDEN TREASURE
DABOO/DAWOO
GIBBERISH GIBBERISH 1, 2, 3
GIBBERISH GIBBERISH A, B, C'S
GIBBERISH GIBBERISH TOUCHING A FLOWER
GIBBERISH GIBBERISH CHASING A SQUIRREL
A BIRD, DISCOVERY OF TREES
GIBBERISH GIBBERISH TEE TEE
RUSHING TO THE BATHROOM
AWAITING GRANDFATHER
TRAINING POTTY IN HAND
SITTING SHE ASKS FOR TOILET PAPER
PLACES IT BEHIND HER LITTLE BUTT
AWAITS
SHE KNOWS THE PROCESS
NOT THE SEQUENCE
ALL ALL
TREASURED MOMENTS IMBEDDED
A MIND RACING TO A TIME LOST LONG AGO

A MOTHER MY WIFE
A SON MY SON
TWIN DAUGHTERS MY DAUGHTERS
A FATHER
TOO BUSY CHASING DREAM AND AMBITION
WITH EASE WITHOUT CARE
WASTED GOLDEN TREASURES
WONDERS OF A DEVELOPING MIND AND BODY
OFFERED
DABOO/DAWOO
NOW TIME
A GRANDFATHER SMILE
HIDES WELL THE SORROW OF LOST TREASURE
OFFERED
CARELESSLY REFUSED
IN A TIME LOST A LONG TIME AGO

ALONE

HIGH UP 20 - 40 THOUSAND FEET
ABOVE
HOT AIR AND COLD AIR
MIXED
CAUSING ELECTRONS TO TAKE SIDES
IT'S MID-MAY 1959
AN UNTYPICAL
COLD FRONT AND WARM FRONT
COLLIDE
CRACKLING LIGHTNING ROLLING THUNDER
MAKES THE SKIN CRAWL WITH STATIC
ELECTRICITY
EARLY IN THE DAY
VERY UNCEREMONIOUS I WAS ASKED TO LEAVE
THE MONASTERY
A CATHOLIC MONK HOUSE
DEDICATED TO THE COMPLETE ABSTINENCE
OF ALL
EARTH PLEASURES
IN THE SERVICE OF GOD
A CULMINATION OF A 9/10 YEAR JOURNEY
MY LIFE SPENT
IN A RELIGIOUS COMPOUND
I LEFT MY HOME IN EARLY YEARS
TO LIVE WITH A CATHOLIC PRIEST
THE MONASTERY WAS AN EASY CHOICE
NOW
AS LIGHTING AND THUNDER PLAY
ALL MEMORIES ARE AWAKENED

LONG LOST AND HIDDEN
BY THE DAILY LOSING BATTLE
TO SERVE GOD
FEAR GUT WRENCHING
FAILURE - AN ANGRY GOD -THE UNKNOWN
FACING SISTER ANDREW
SHE WOULD SOON CONDEMN ME TO HELL
RAIN FALLING
THUNDER AND LIGHTING IN A CONTINUOUS
FIGHT
A SMALL CANOPY MY ONLY SHELTER
THE DOOR TO THE MONASTERY LOCKED
I WAS ONE OF THEM NO MORE
WAITING TO BE PICKED UP
COUNTING CAR HEAD LIGHTS
PRAYING FOR HELP
ABANDONED NO HELP IN SIGHT
A 17 YEAR OLD WITH FEARS AND DOUBT
OF A 17TH CENTURY CHRISTIAN
HELL AND SATAN ARE REAL
I CAN FEEL THEM AND SEE THEM
A WARPED MIND

CREEPY

WHEN MY BODY IN A GRAVE DOES LIE
AND MY SOUL WITH TIME FLIES
IT WILL BE TIME FOR THE WORM TO COME
ONE AT FIRST BUT THERE'LL BE MORE
SLOWLY THEY WILL EAT ME BACK TO DIRT
I WILL RETURN TO MOTHER EARTH
NINE MONTHS FOR ME TO BE
A NEWBORN BABY
FACING LIFE AND ITS MISERIES
NOW HERE I LAY DOWN IN THE GROUND
WITH WORMS ALL AROUND
BE GENTLE YOU DIRTY CREATURES
TRY NOT TO DISGRACE MY LOVELY FEATURES
LIVE AND TRY NOT TO BE A CLOWN
REMEMBERING WHAT AWAITS
DOWN IN THE GROUND

THOUGHTS ON A SUNDAY MORNING
AT THE CROSS ROAD CHURCH
WHILE VISITING MARSHALL, TX

THE REVERBERATING ECHOES
WITHIN THE SANCTUARY
AS A FEW HUNDRED SANG SILENT NIGHT
IN CELEBRATION OF THE HOLIDAYS APPROACHING
MY EYES CAUGHT BY THE CONTRASTING SIGHT
OF A WOODEN CROSS
A REMEMBRANCE OF A DIFFERENT CELEBRATION
                    SILENT NIGHT HOLY NIGHT
A BETRAYER AMONG THE MIDST
A QUESTION ASKED BY HIS TRIBE
                    ALL IS CALM ALL IS BRIGHT
WHO ARE YOU
A KING   YOUNG ROUND VIRGIN
I AM WHO I AM
                    MOTHER AND CHILD
BLASPHEMER LAW BREAKER
A KING
                    HOLY INFANT
PONTIUS PILOT
A HELPING HAND
                    SO TENDER AND MILD
A KING A KING OF THE JEWS
SECOND THOUGHTS DOUBTS
WON'T TAKE NO FOR AN ANSWER
                    SLEEP IN HEAVENLY PEACE

TWO CRIMINALS
CHOOSE ONE
JESUS
                    SLEEP IN HEAVENLY PEACE
SCOURGED CROWN OF THORNS
RIPPED SKINS MINGLED WITH BLOOD
A WHIP MEETING FLESH
WHO WINS
                    SILENT NIGHT HOLY NIGHT
   PRESENTED TO HIS PEOPLE
CHEERS AND JEERS
DEATH DEATH TO THE
                    ALL IS CLAM ALL IS BRIGHT
IMPOSTER
A KING OF JEW   HOLY NIGHT
DEATH ON A WOODEN CROSS
                    HOLY HOLY

LIFE A JOKE

I THINK I'LL DIE TODAY
THERE IS NO REASON FOR ME TO STAY
CLOUDS OF HATE HAVE LOST ME MY WAY
I LEARN I CRY
MOST OF ALL I WISH TO DIE
I THINK I'LL DIE TODAY
THERE IS NO REASON FOR ME TO STAY
SPEAK YOUR MIND I'LL LISTEN TO WHAT YOU
HAVE TO SAY
MIND YOU I'LL RATHER DIE TODAY
THERE IS NO REASON FOR ME TO STAY
THIS WORLD I'VE SEEN AND IT'S NO DREAM
I RATHER DIE TODAY
I THINK I'LL DIE TODAY
THERE IS NO REASON FOR ME TO STAY
THIS WORLD A STAGE AND I ITS CLOWN
NO THANK YOU I RATHER NOT STAY AROUND
I THINK I'LL DIE TODAY
THERE IS NO REASON FOR ME TO STAY

TIRED

SOMETIMES MY DAYS SEEM A LITTLE LONG
SOMETIMES MY JOB IS A LITTLE HEAVIER
AT TIMES I FEEL LIKE SKIPPING OUT
THEN I THINK OF MY WIFE AND CHILDREN
THE SUM WORTH OF MY LIFE
HEADLINES PREDICT
ANOTHER WAR
SOARING CRIME
HALF THE WORLD STARVING
WHILE YOU AND I WORRY
HOW MANY DOLLARS WE CAN MAKE
IF IT WASN'T FOR MY WIFE AND CHILDREN
LIFE WOULD NOT BE WORTH MY WHILE
EVERYDAY THERE IS A DEMONSTRATION
EVERYONE SEEKING MORE ATTENTION
WHILE THE OTHER HALF IS DYING
IN SOMEONE'S WAR

THE SACRIFICED LAMB

YOU HAVE SEEN THE PICTURES
THE TORN FLESH RIPPED
APART BY WHIPS
BLOOD DRIPPING
LIKE HONEY
FROM THE THORNS DUG INTO FLESH
A CROWN
THE HAMMERED SPIKES
BINDING HANDS AND FEET
TO ROUGHEN WOOD
THE MOCKING SIGN
PROCLAIMING TO ALL
THE KING OF JEWS
THE GOD SON A SAVIOR
THE SAVIOR
A MEMORY
OF A TIME LONG AGO
THE WARNING SIGNS WERE AMPLE
CAUTION WAS THROWN TO THE WIND
THE HUMAN SENSES
SIGHT HEARING TASTE SMELL AND TOUCH
ALL
A BOTHERSOME CRUTCH
SOMETIMES
A FIGHT WAS FOUGHT
GOOD AND EVIL
EVIL WON
A STUMBLE
IN THE LIFE OF A SINNER
THE TIME OF LONG AGO
A TORTURED FACE WRECKED IN PAIN
A SUBDUED FROWN A WINCE
UNNOTICED
ACKNOWLEDGES ONCE AGAIN
THE ADDED PAIN OF
A NEXT SIN

© copyright 2010 Jesse Carreon

THE CRUCIFIXION

THE BEAUTY OF HER FACE WAS MADE OPAQUE BY
HER SENSUAL BODY CURVES
ACCENTUATED BY THE BLACK DRESS
HER CLEVERNESS AND INTELLIGENCE
WELL HIDDEN
BEHIND HER EARTHLY SEXUALITY
THE FARAWAY DING OF A CROWD
BROUGHT A FAINT SMILE (A LA MONA LISA)
UNLEASHING HIDDEN DEMONIC FORCES AWAKE
   NOT UNLIKE THOSE SEEN IN THE MOTION PICTURE
   INDIANA JONES AND THE LAST CRUSADE
CREATING A ZONE OF EVIL
IN PREPARATION FOR THE DEATH HUNGRY CROWD
AS IT APPROACHED IT DESTINATION POINT
SHE ZOOMED UNSEEN UNTO THE CROWD
THE BLACK DRESS BEAUTY AND HER COMPANIONS
AGITATING THE NEGATIVE ELECTRONS
CREATING AN ATMOSPHERE
WHERE THE HATE OF ALL TIME MINGLED WITH
THE STINKS OF HUMANITY HUMAN STRESS AND
SHOUTS OF THE WORLD
THE ABSENCE OF FEAR
OPENED THE GATES OF HELL GIVING LEEWAY
TO A OPEN VORTEX OF HATE CENTERED
ALL EVIL SPRITS UNLEASHED TO THIS ONE SPOT
GOGATH... THE SKULL PLACE
ALL JOINING IN ONE COMMON CAUSE
THE MURMUR AND SHOUTING BUILDING
INTO A CRESCENDO OF CLEAR WORDS

CRUCIFY HIM CRUCIFY HIM CRUCIFY HIM
THE KING OF JEWS A KING THE KING
YES
THERE WERE A FEW TEARS
A FEW BROKEN HEARTS
ALL HIDDEN AND SUBDUED
BY FEAR
A COSMIC PICTURE OF MANKIND
BLIND TO THE WILL OF THE CREATOR
AS THE CRUCIFIED ONE CRIED
IT IS FINISHED IT IS FINISHED
A WILD CELEBRATING PROCESSION
COULD BE SEEN
HEADED BY THE LADY IN BLACK
AND HER EARTHLY SERVILE MINIONS

TOMORROW

WHEN TOMORROW COMES
　　　　　WILL THE SUN SHINE
WHEN TOMORROW COMES
　　　　　WILL THE STARS TWINKLE
　　　　　AS THEY DO TONIGHT
WHEN TOMORROW COMES
　　　　　WILL THE MORNING DEW
　　　　　QUENCH MOTHER EARTH
WHEN TOMORROW COMES
　　　　　WILL THE BIRDS SING
WHEN TOMORROW COMES
　　　　　WILL THE DOGS BARK AND
　　　　　THE CHILDREN SCREAM
WHEN TOMORROW COMES
　　　　　WILL WE BE ALIVE
WHEN TOMORROW COMES
　　　　　WILL WE BE MEMORIES
WHEN TOMORROW COMES
WHEN TOMORROW COMES

COLOR FLOWERS

SEE
THE FLOWERS SHINE
BEAUTIFUL COLORS
RUNNING PAST MY MIND
I FEEL MYSELF
CARRIED TO THE END OF TIME
BLUE IS PLEASING TO THE EYE
WHITE IS FOR THE PURE OF HEART
RED IS FOR THE BRAVE AND STRONG
VIOLET IS FOR THE HOT TEMPERED FOOL
SEE THE FLOWERS ALL ALONE
BEAUTIFUL FLOWERS
IF I COULD BE ONE OF YOU
I LIKE TO BE THE COLOR BLUE

DALLAS AT 2:30 PM SAT AFTERNOON 1974

THE FLASHING "DON'T WALK"
SIGNAL
BROKE THE TRANCE
MAN MADE STRUCTURES OF CONCRETE AND
STEEL
SEEM TO COME ALIVE
I LOOKED SEARCHING
HUMAN COMPANIONSHIP MY NEED
360 DEGREES FAR AS I COULD SEE
NO ONE
I STOOD ALONE
CLICK CLICK HUM HUM HONK HONK
I STOOD SURROUNDED BY THESE
MECHANICAL MONSTERS
GEN CUSTER MUST HAVE FELT THE SAME
THE COLD WIND CUT INTO MY BODY
AS IF I WAS NAKED
IN UNISON THEY SPOKE
WOO' WOO' BUSS' BUSS'
CLICK' CLICK' HUMM' HUMM'
ALL FOREIGN TONGUES
NONE I COULD UNDERSTAND
I APOLOGIZED FOR BEING HUMAN
OH
IF I COULD BE A VOLKSWAGEN
FEAR AND DESPERATION
FORCED ME TO CRY OUT
'KEMO SABE' 'KEMO SABE'
LONE RANGER WHERE ARE YOU

ONE MILLION EYES
ONE MILLION VOICES
ONE MILLION HANDS
COLD
ALL MADE OF STEEL GLASS AND CEMENT
MY BODY WAS IN TURMOIL
MY MIND WAS IN TURMOIL
MY SOUL WAS IN TURMOIL
ALL RACING
IN 3 DIFFERENT DIRECTIONS
I WAS ALONE
LONELINESS
CAN HURT

A FUNERAL IN THE 1950'S

MEMORIES OF THE FUNERAL ITSELF
FORGOTTEN DRIFTWOOD ON A BEACH
THE NEW CAR SMELL IS WELL REMEMBERED
A STUDEBAKER BRAND NEW
TWO TONE
FIRST NEW CAR I EVER BEEN IN
A RIDE HOME FOR
A POOR MEXICAN BOY FROM WEST DALLAS
THE AFTERNOON SUN BRIGHT AND HOT
NO HINT THAT A LIFE
MY LIFE
WAS AT A TURNING POINT
SISTER DOLORES AND SISTER MALTILDA
CATHOLIC NUNS
FATHER SEBASTION
A CATHOLIC PRIEST
I HAD HELPED WITH THE FUNERAL SERVICE
AN ALTAR BOY
NOTHING NEW
I HAD ASSISTED MANY TIMES BEFORE
A DUTY FOR AN ALTAR BOY
DUTY FINISHED
ON MY WAY HOME
A FREE RIDE
SAVED MY BUS MONEY 10 CENTS
I DO NOT REMEMBER WHO
NOR WHY
SOMEONE MENTIONED

TIME COULD BE SAVED
IF I
LIVED NEAR BY
HIGH IN THE SKY A BLACK BIRD
FLYING SOLO A WARNING
FUNNY HOW INTUITION IS REAL
MY BODY WARNED ME
THAT SILENT VOICE TUGGING MY HEART
FEAR EXCITEMENT
HOW
CAN AN 8 YEAR OLD MIND
DEDUCE SO MUCH FROM A BIRD IN THE SKY
I KNEW MY LIFE WAS ABOUT TO CHANGE
NO CONTROL LIFE CRUISING ON AUTO PILOT
NOT MUCH MORE IS REMEMBERED
TWO DAYS LATER I LEFT MY HOME
8 YEARS OLD
TO LIVE AT THE PRIEST RECTORY
I WOULD NOT RETURN
UNTIL THE FALL OF MY 17TH YEAR

CONFUSED

I, "WHO ARE YOU?"
YOU "I AM HE"
HE "HE IS I"
I, YOU AND HE "WE ARE ONE ANOTHER, THEREFORE ONE"
THEY "THEY ARE WRONG, I AM ONE"
I, YOU AND HE "NO! WE ARE ONE"
THEY "NO! NO! I AM ONE, THEREFORE ANOTHER"
I, YOU, HE AND THEY "WE ARE ONE WE ARE TWO. WE ARE MORE. WHO ARE WE??
WE DON'T KNOW"

Printed in the United States
By Bookmasters